RUNNING YOUR FIRST MARATHON MADE EASY

RUNNING YOUR FIRST MARATHON MADE EASY

ALL THE SECRETS YOU NEED TO KNOW FOR FIRST MARATHON SUCCESS

JOHN MCDONNELL

This book is dedicated to Carleth Keys. Carleth is a social media influencer in the sphere of running. She embodies everything that the world of marathon running requires. Among these qualities are strength, courage, perseverance and a willingness to spread the joy that the sport of running brings to so many people. She spends much of her time in Spain, as do I these days, and it has been a great pleasure to share the miles around Madrid and chatting about the sport we both love.

DISCLAIMER

Keeping physically active is key to maintaining a healthy lifestyle. But it is always best to check with your doctor before taking part in any sport, like running, to ensure it is safe for you to do so. Although you may be an experienced runner already, please ensure you get clearance from your doctor as the intensity of some of these workouts are quite high.

First published in 2024 by Greative Books Publishing, Ltd.
Grogey Road
Fivemiletown
Tyrone
BT750NT

Copyright © John McDonnell, 2024

The moral right of the author has been asserted

Every effort has been made to trace copyright holders and to obtain their permission for the use of copyrighted material. The publisher apologizes for any errors or omissions and would be grateful if notified of any corrections that should be incorporated in future reprints of this book.

All rights reserved.

No part of this publication may be reproduced, stored in a retrieval system, or transmitted in any form or by any means, electronic, mechanical, photocopying, recording or otherwise, without the prior written permission from the author or the publishers, except for the use of brief quotations in a book review.

Book Cover Design: Owen McDonnell & Thea Chetcuti

Edited by Roisin McDonnell

ISBN Paperback: 9781739547127
ISBN Ebook: 9781739547134

ABOUT THE AUTHOR

John McDonnell is a UK Athletics Coach in Running Fitness. He has written several books on running as well as his memoir describing how the sport of running saved his life.

At the age of 48, he was a healthy and fit marathon runner who was progressing in the sport on a personal level and had been coaching other runners for three years. Then, out of the blue, he suffered a stroke. It turned out to be caused by an 11mm hole in his heart. He had heart surgery, called an ASD closure, later that same year. It was however, the sport of running that ensured he was strong enough to return to life, relatively close to the same as he was before the stroke.

It was the coaching of other runners that kept his sanity during the months of rehab and no racing. Needless to say, running has defined John for many years now and continues to do so today. He has built his brand around A Heart for Running and you can view his personal and coaching content by clicking the links below (ebook only).

He also hosts much of his coaching content on Achieve Running Club social media accounts. The Achieve Running Club is a free support network of runners for runners. Please reach out at any of his social media outlets as John is keen to help runners achieve their running goals, whatever they may be.

CONTENTS

Introduction	xv
1. GETTING READY TO BEGIN	1
Running My First Marathon & Finding Inspiration	1
Your Turn	8
2. DECIDE ON YOUR GOALS	11
3. DETERMINE WHAT YOU ARE WILLING TO DO	14
4. ESTIMATED RACE FINISH TIME	18
5. RUNNING SHOES & GEAR	22
Running Gear	28
Lessons to take away regarding shoes & gear:	29
6. ADVICE AND WHAT I WISH SOMEONE TOLD ME BEFORE I FOUND OUT FOR MYSELF	31
Stretching	31
Chafing	35
Eating Before Race Day	38
In Race Fueling	41
Arriving to the Starting Line	44
Pacing	45
Missed Sessions	48
Injuries	50
Be Careful Who You Listen to	55
Lessons to take away:	57
7. A CASE STUDY IN OVERCOMING INJURY	59
8. A REVIEW OF RUNNING TECHNIQUE & BEST PRACTICES	62
Running Form & Technique	62
Pre-Session Dynamics	68

9. PHYSICAL PREPARATION	69
Aerobic Conditioning	70
Strength Training	71
Heart Rate (Pulse Rate)	75
Resting Heart Rate	76
Sleep	76
Nutrition & Hydration	78
Carbohydrates	79
Protein	80
Fats	81
Hydration	82
Electrolytes	84
Preparing Nutritionally for Race Day	85
Gels & In Race Nutrition	87
Caffeine	89
Alcohol	90
10. MENTAL PREPARATION	91
11. A CASE STUDY IN OVERCOMING SELF-DOUBT	94
12. WHAT TO DO IN THE DAYS BEFORE THE MARATHON	97
The Expo	98
Walking & Touring	98
Bag Drop & Throw Aways	98
To Run with a Pacer or Not	100
Post Race Meeting Point	101
Race Day Preparations	101
The Race	102

THE TRAINING PLAN FOR FIRST MARATHON SUCCESS

THE TRAINING PLAN	107
THE BASE LOADING PHASE	114
Week 1	114
Week 2	118

Week 3	121
Week 4	123
THE BASE BUILDING PHASE	127
Week 5	128
Week 6	131
Week 7	134
Week 8	136
THE PACE PHASE	140
Week 9 (Cutback Week – Yay!)	141
Week 10	144
Week 11	148
Week 12	151
Week 13 (Another Cutback Week!)	153
Week 14	156
Week 15	159
Week 16	161
THE RACE PHASE	164
Week 17	165
Week 18	168
Week 19	171
Week 20	175
POST RACE CARE	178
Congratulations	181
Personal Coaching	185
Acknowledgments	187
Also by John McDonnell	189

INTRODUCTION

So, somebody convinced you to run your first marathon? Who was it and what did you do that made them want to punish you with such an endeavor? Whatever the reason, you find yourself here, seeking guidance from an experienced coach. Searching for some help to somehow figure out how you are going to manage to move your body 26.2 miles forward over the course of several hours. All of this without collapsing in a heap along the way.

Well, I'm here to tell you that not only can you accomplish this, but you can do it and enjoy the entire event. I will also say that you can complete this and come out the other side a more powerful, self-confident and otherwise emotionally and physically stronger individual. This is because marathon running isn't for the faint-hearted. It is every bit a test of will, from the first day a runner begins this quest. And the quest begins 20 weeks before race day. There will be ups and downs; good days and bad; laughter and tears. It is like

INTRODUCTION

anything in life that is worth doing. That's the thing though, it's a lot of work, but it's worth it. The moment you cross the finish line in your first marathon, you are a marathoner and nobody can ever take that away from you. It is a badge of honor and a label proving you possess an abundance of strength and courage. I give you credit for making the decision to follow it through.

There is something about facing down 26.2 miles, and conquering each one of them, that builds character, mental strength, and self-belief. The first time we do anything that we once thought we were incapable of is a building block in our personal development. Success in the marathon leads to success in other aspects of our lives. Goals will seem much more achievable. Whether it is losing weight, seeking a new career, finding a life partner, building wealth, nothing will seem impossible.

You don't need to have the confidence to start, as a matter of fact, few of us did. A marathon runner isn't born until they have crossed that finish line. We all doubted ourselves until that point. But crossing that threshold is life-changing. The feeling of monumental achievement is hard to overestimate. For many first-time marathon runners, a wave of tears starts to flow the moment that line is crossed as the emotions kick in. For others, it may take a couple of hours or even days to fully appreciate it and realize just how amazing this task was, but it always does. I know it's a bit cliche, but not many marathoners will finish a race and not tell everyone who will listen what they just did. It is an achievement worthy of being proud of.

INTRODUCTION

So why is it such an achievement; it's only a long run? Well, for starters, you don't just rock up to your first marathon and jump in. You have to prepare for months ahead of time. It takes up to 20 weeks to properly train for your first marathon. Of course, it really depends on your starting point and your level of fitness, but let's just say 20 weeks. That's five months of consistent training, healthy eating, prioritizing sleep and a positive mental approach. If you manage to get through those weeks and months of training preparing for one morning's long run, you best be damn sure you appreciate the effort come race day. You deserve all the pride and awesomeness that comes with that finishers medal.

Depending on the time of year the marathon is taking place, you will likely not only battle your own mind, but Mother Nature herself. If you are preparing for a spring marathon, be prepared for early morning runs, dark evenings, cold and wet runs and discomfort on levels you may never have thought possible. (Am I doing a good job selling this)?

As for the race itself, all experienced marathon runners have their horror stories describing one disastrous race or another. One of the objectives of this book will be to help you avoid such an experience. I include here many lessons learned and subtle tips and advice for new marathon runners that you will find invaluable come race day. Take onboard all the many years of experience and don't make these same mistakes. Let my pain be your lesson.

The fact of the matter is that completing the distance is a straight-forward journey. The advice included in this book

INTRODUCTION

will guide you through the process, step-by-step. If you read the entire book, it will all be laid out in front of you, right down to when to cut your toenails. Your first marathon is not only achievable, but the process is easy to follow. I am confident that you won't regret taking this on.

CHAPTER 1
GETTING READY TO BEGIN

RUNNING MY FIRST MARATHON & FINDING INSPIRATION

Deciding you want to run a marathon is quite the individual experience. For me, I started running in order to lose weight and improve my overall health and wellbeing. Back in 2010, at the age of 42, I returned home from a family vacation and when we went through the photographs, the one thing that struck me was how overweight I looked. Becoming overweight isn't something that occurs overnight. It is a slow process. Day after day, week after week, recklessly eating without considering what I was consuming. Maybe it was years of growing up without really needing to worry about my weight. Maybe because I had a complete lack of knowledge of nutrition. Sure, we all *think* we know what is healthy and what is unhealthy, but do we really? I never really considered it too much. Additionally, from the age of 15, I had a fondness for beer, wine and whisky. I even smoked cigarettes until the age of 28, and beyond that, on a part-time basis.

My wife and I have four kids and, as it happens, their lives started taking over from our own, and time was at a premium. We also had a new business that was starting to pick up steam. Health and fitness weren't my top priority. Needless to say, the pounds started to pack on and after seeing these photos, I knew I needed to start taking my health a little more seriously. That's when it all began.

I started out running alongside my wife. After running for a few months, we signed up for our first organized 5k. I literally had no idea what to expect. I was still overweight, but I was confident I could run the 5k distance. It turned out to be so much harder than I ever could have imagined, but we managed to complete the distance in a respectable time. It wasn't so unpleasant that it put me off my training and before long I signed up for a 10k. What I didn't know was that this local 10k was being run over an extremely difficult course, climbing a ridiculously long and steep hill. Once again, having only been running less than a year, I struggled, but I finished this 10k. For me, it was the post-race hospitality that really made the incredibly difficult race all worth it. Being a winter race in Ireland it was cold, so the post-race hot soup, coffee and sandwiches, as well as cakes and biscuits, made the hard effort a distant memory. It also brought together a large running community, of which I relished being a part. I continued to run for the next year or so, training a little less, as our business steadily grew.

As the training went on over the winter months of 2011 and into the spring of 2012, I set my sights on a half-marathon. That spring, I got over that hurdle in a much larger event than the previous two. I was impressed with the entire experience, particularly the buzz on the start line with thousands of other runners. There was a camaraderie among the participants of all abilities. Personally, I was growing in confidence as a runner and thoroughly proud of myself as I continued to improve my fitness. The weight loss was a bonus, and by November of 2012 my weight was down 45 pounds. I had literally transformed my body and actually needed a new wardrobe. I also got to know more and more runners. There is something about runners that brings out the best in all of us. I'm not sure if it is the shared experience of doing hard things, or the fact that running is one of the most mentally demanding sports, but runners have a little something special. They are generally positive people to be around.

After this particular half marathon, I put serious thought into a full marathon and by winter of 2012, along with my wife, I had signed up for the Belfast City Marathon. How exciting and scary. This was our first full marathon, and we set out to train to cover 26.2 miles. Armed with next to no knowledge on how to train for a marathon, we sought advice from those we knew who had completed one. We didn't know many, but still, managed to get some of the basics. We slowly increased our weekly long run and our total weekly miles, which was excellent advice. We also learned about taking gels on long runs, which was new to us.

The race date for Belfast was May 6th. However, by mid-February I felt I was ready and wanted to try to run a full marathon. This was a personal challenge for me and me alone. Did I have what it takes to be a marathoner? So, I did what so many runners do. I sat at my computer and searched for races. I found one that was taking place the following week. I contacted the organizers and managed to get myself a place on short notice. It was a small, rural marathon in the west of Ireland in a town called Sixmilebridge.

Full of excitement, and plenty of anxiety, I left work early on the Friday before the Saturday race and drove myself down to County Clare where I stayed the night in a local hotel. I was told that I was supposed to "carb-up" that night before, so for dinner I had pasta, garlic bread and a pint of Guinness. I figured this would work well enough. I know I have a pretty hearty stomach for most foods and gave it very little thought.

Waking early the next morning, I made myself some instant oatmeal in my hotel room, but, similar to my evening meal, I didn't overthink breakfast either. I actually didn't know that I needed to. One area of complaint many runners have is making sure they can empty their bowels before their event. This has proven not to be an area of concern for me as usually a cup of coffee and I'm good to go, literally. This morning, it was much the same. Before long I nervously got into my running gear; shorts, socks, shoes, band-aids, t-shirt, jacket, gloves, and hat and drove out to the registration area where I introduced myself to a few of the participants and picked up my race bib. I don't exactly recall what I was expecting, but this was a very small event, with a field of only 35 runners. The intimacy of the event really took the pressure off and on the way around the undulating course I got to talk to a number of the runners. Without exception, each one I talked to had helpful advice and shared their own experiences with me. It is a recurring theme. Runners are super people, full of support for one another. One of the most memorable aspects of the day, the awesome fellow runners aside, was that the weather was remarkably clear and pleasantly cool. The west of Ireland can be quite brutal in the winter months, year-round honestly, but the day cooperated the best it could. No wind to contend with. No rain to weigh me down. It was just a very nice day in County Clare.

I was asked before the start what my target was. I wasn't sure, as it was my first time, but I thought I could manage a 10-minute mile pace. I had no sports watch and wasn't running with a phone and therefore, had no way to tell what my pace was. The first half of the event went rather well, reaching the 13.1-mile mark at 2:08:20. I found a rhythm, a constant and steady beat of my feet hitting the ground. This felt like all of the long training runs that I ran in the months leading up to the day. I didn't try to do anything I wasn't capable of. There was no chance of falling into the overconfidence trap that trips up many first-time marathoners. Many runners feel fresh around the midway point and start to think, "this is easy. I can run much faster than this and I could finish under four hours if I really push myself." If I had, the likelihood was high of a big crash and the end of my running life there and then.

The second half, well, there's no way it could be described as *enjoyable*, but it wasn't torture either. One stride after the next, a relentless and seemingly never-ending march towards the finish. I definitely slowed down over the course of the second 13.1. Reaching the finish line in one piece, not hobbling or injured, the clock read 4:22:58. My first marathon was completed and, somehow, my target of 10 minutes per mile was hit, very nearly spot on. To be honest, it wasn't really a goal pace or goal time. It was something I had been asked about in the morning. I would have been happy to just finish it without dying.

I received my medal alongside a boat load of congratulations from many of the others who ran on the day, each recalling their first marathon. I was told over and over how addictive marathon running was, and for me personally, it turned out to be true, as I would go on to run three more that year. I completed my 40th official marathon in April 2024, each one another life-lesson.

I'd like to say that running a marathon was a bucket list item for me. Or that all I ever wanted to do was run the Boston Marathon, London, or New York. But my first marathon was simply a culmination of enjoying my weight-loss and fitness process and wanting to challenge myself. It was as simple as that. Nobody ever dared me to do one. Nobody ever said I couldn't. I just thought I could do it and wanted to prove to myself that I could. However, since that day in County Clare, my passion for marathon running has taken hold. It is my belief that for many of you, your first marathon will be the first of many, no matter how you feel about it today. If you do it right, put in the training and pursue it with your own *why*, you will never look back and you certainly won't ever regret it.

Later that same year I witnessed something that inspired me to take up coaching. On the 3rd of June I ran the Cork City Marathon. This was my third marathon within four months and I was planning on pushing myself to run faster than I did in my first two. I set myself a goal of finishing under 4 hours. At the time, this was a tough challenge and I was unsure if it was going to be possible. Once again, the weather played ball and gave us a clear, sunny day with no wind to contend with. I was grateful to run once again with many from the Marathon Club Ireland who ran with me in Sixmilebridge four months earlier.

I had a great run on the day and everything went to plan crossing the line with a chip time of 3:57:40. I left it all out there on the streets of Cork and was spent at the finish. Unfortunately, there was a two mile walk to get to the bag drop and then back to the hotel. There was also a monumental drive ahead of me to contend with so there was no hanging about to celebrate. Walking was difficult and I looked rather like the tin-man from the Wizard of Oz. It's so funny, and relatable, that it is exactly how all the TV commercials portray the condition of runners post-marathon.

I eventually managed to get back to the hotel where I showered, checked out, and loaded up the car. The trip back home took me across the marathon route. One of the more unforgettable scenes for me was when we saw one individual still on the course. She had about a mile or so to go and it was over the six-hour mark since the start. To me this was inspirational. That effort was far more impressive than most of us on the course on that day. Here was someone who decided to take on the challenge and decided she wasn't going to give up. She persevered and finished what was a massive accomplishment. I thought that hers was the kind of spirit that needed to be shared. I wanted to spread that passion, that grit and determination to as many people as I could. From that point on I started studying, watching, and taking notes about the sport and the great runners we are lucky enough to have in this world. Two years later I passed my coaching qualification and the rest is history. I've been doing my best to bring that one woman's passion to as many people as possible and it has been a genuinely awesome experience for me. I enjoy coaching and I'm so grateful to be able to do it.

YOUR TURN

So, what about you? The decision has been made, you've either been bullied into it or you are just damned determined to prove something to yourself, (hopefully the latter). You are running your first marathon. Ideally, you've purchased this book at least 20-weeks before arriving at the start line. But even if the event is sooner, you got this. One of the many things a first-time marathon runner needs to consider is what exactly they are signing up to. This is, at the very least, a four-month commitment to a training program that will entail running consistently 5 days per week. Much of this will be running long distances, slowly building your weekly mileage and your weekly long run. If you are coming from a 5k-10k background or even a half-marathon or two, the weekly mileage will likely seem significantly more.

This commitment in time is substantial. If you have a young family, this is something that will need to be taken into consideration. Ensure you discuss this with your partner and that you have the support you require going into week one. It can't be underestimated the sacrifice the people around you may be making. If you have that support network, this will be remarkably easier. If, on the other hand, you find yourself having to train around everyone else's schedule all the time, that might just mean that the timing isn't right. However, if it is important to you, you will make it happen. Know your *why*.

Some of the considerations that will need to be made, besides the time commitment, include costs, overall soreness, mountains of laundry, and the general feeling of transforming into something even more amazing than you once were. For the most part, the first three things can be mitigated against, except the third, as that is just unavoidable.

As far as costs go, most marathons these days don't come cheap. It may be a valid question, why would I pay so much money in order to punish myself. Well, to be honest, it does seem a bit crazy on the surface. I am not here to defend different race organizers, but there are a lot of costs that go into putting on a race of 26.2 miles and organizers must pass these on to the participants. There are simply too many to post a full list here, but consider the cost to close down the roads of a city for half a day. There is water and other nutritional stops along the way, as well as medals and t-shirts. The list is long.

But for the participant, like you, there is the cost of transportation, accommodation, food, running shoes, running clothes and much more to consider. There will be costs for the self-care that will be needed over the next few months like sports massages, gym memberships, physio appointments, yoga classes, etc. Many of these can be done inexpensively, but the point is that there may be quite a bit more to take into consideration than you might think.

CHAPTER 2
DECIDE ON YOUR GOALS

For a great many people, the majority perhaps, the accomplishment of running and finishing a marathon, as a personal challenge, is the goal. A "respectable" time, whatever that is in your mind, would be great, but completing a race of 26.2 miles is a mountain that many people have on their bucket list to climb. This is an overriding theme I hear from most of the first-time marathoners that I coach. It is also a goal I wholeheartedly recommend to the vast majority of first-timers. I coach them to finish the marathon, feeling strong and to enjoy the experience as a whole. Not just race day, but the incredible journey from the moment they pulled the trigger on the decision to run one.

The entire training block, be it 16 weeks, 20 weeks, or somewhere in between will be a learning experience. It will be transformational. Starting out as a normal human being and coming out the other side as a marathoner is nothing to be scoffed at. I don't think anyone comes through the program without a new found self-confidence and self-belief. To start out full of doubt, work hard for a few months and accomplish something that before you started seemed impossible, well that is metamorphic. And if you think I'm overstating the process, there's only one way to prove me wrong. Go out and do it.

It only seems impossible until it is broken down into small chunks. It's like any other process, say building a house. It takes someone who has done it before to see an empty field and can envision the house at its conclusion, standing tall and strong against the horizon. When the process begins it's just a jumble of lines on a big sheet of paper. Soon, the first machines arrive to clear the land, it begins to feel like progress is being made. The house is lined out, pipes and plumbing are laid in preparation for the foundation. Then foundations get poured, more progress. The walls go up, then the roof, plumbing, and electrical wiring is installed. It takes time, but eventually, the house that was just a thought becomes a reality.

Building a marathon runner follows a similar path. At first it is just an idea, "I'd love to run a marathon, but it would be impossible. I'm not a real runner." I'm here to tell you that if you run, you are a runner. Taking the decision to run a marathon isn't something one takes lightly. Once you've committed to the end goal, the fun begins. Keep an open mind, embrace the challenge and you will never look back. Your marathoning body is built and completed over the course of this process, much like the house. You may not be able to see it just yet, but trust your training. Trust your coach, listen to the advice in this book. Do the required work and I promise you will walk taller and be stronger when you cross that finish line.

So, let's start by making the assumption that your goal is to complete the distance and enjoy the experience. You can follow the plan for this goal. To complete and enjoy. This is an admirable and pretty epic result for any first-time marathoner. Does it matter how long it takes? I suggest no, it does not. Can you still run a respectable time? Of course you can, but the target is to finish and smile, (or break down in tears of joy like you just won the lottery).

The plan included in this book will work just as well if you have a finish time in mind. I offer a race time predictor in an upcoming chapter that will help you decide what pace you will need to run based on your finish times in shorter distances. The plan is relative to the runner, so whatever ability you are, that will be the pace to run.

I have spent the last few years refining my training log template that I use for my own training. These have been made available on the Achieve Running Club website. The Google Sheets, or the alternative Excel Spreadsheets, for the plan included in this book, is available at a 50% discount for purchaser's of this book. You can find this training log at https://jmruncoach.com. Just use Discount Code: **RYFM_50** on checkout to receive your price reduction.

CHAPTER 3
DETERMINE WHAT YOU ARE WILLING TO DO

What is happening in your life? Can you fit 5 months of dedicated running training into your schedule? It can certainly add to your stress. On the other hand, running can be a huge stress relief outlet for many people. So, what are you willing and able to do? This is an important question. Marathon training consists of sacrifices. These sacrifices are yours to bear, but also the burden of everyone around you. Friends and family may feel like you are putting the marathon ahead of them. They may feel less important as you focus on your own personal goal for once. However, if this is something that you are passionately chasing, then do whatever it is that you have to do. Commit and you will not regret it.

However, you may have limitations put upon you by your other life commitments like work, children, other responsibilities. In this case, determine how many days a week you are able to train. Once you know that, the training regime can be built around it. So, for example, I've coached a marathon runner who only had three days per week available for training. This is, ultimately, the fewest number of days I would recommend for a marathon training program. It can be done, and it can be executed quite successfully. Knowing this limitation is important before beginning any program.

It is of great importance to have an agreement with everyone affected by your commitment to training as to who will take on what responsibilities. If you are a primary caregiver to someone, then ensure that someone will be there to take your place over the next four to five months. For example, if you have school runs to arrange with other parents, just ensure you've thought this through.

Also, if you do shift work, that can lead to challenges as well. It will be important that you understand that there are simply some weekly runs that cannot be missed on a consistent basis, no matter what. Your weekly long run, whatever day of the week it is possible for you to complete it, must be completed. Sure, it won't be the end of your training if you miss one or two, but miss four or five and you will likely feel the difference and the experience will be diminished on race day. It may feel much harder than it needs to.

Ideally, there won't be any limitations on how often you can train. In this case, flexibility can be used to create a program that encompasses a more diverse and therefore less intensive training regime. This is highly advantageous for the first-time marathon runner. In the long run, this will open up more of an opportunity to complete the marathon, feeling strong and less worn down by the 26.2-mile event. The better you feel at the end, ultimately, the more enjoyable the experience, and therefore, the more likely you will wish to do it again. This may not be your goal whatsoever. You may say, "no way, this is a one-shot deal. I will do this marathon, but never again!" I say you may be surprised how you feel when you complete it. There is a tendency to go back, again and again. I know it may not seem like it now, but just wait. Never say never.

Another variable that needs to be taken into consideration is what time of year do you want to run your marathon? If you choose a spring marathon then you will be training through the winter months. For most, this will include training through some inclement weather. Maybe some snow, rain, wind and cold. Although it sounds awful, this can add to the challenge. It really depends on your personality. Are you someone who is prepared to do whatever it takes to complete this mission? Or, do you want to get through it and hope for the most advantageous training weather window. If you are in the latter category, then choose wisely which marathon race you sign up to. Obviously, a summer marathon where you live may be out of the question due to extreme heat. All I'm saying is make a deliberate decision and understand that the weather has a lot to say when it comes to one's enjoyment in training. Some of us like to feel a little more hardcore, thus winter training isn't a bad thing. Some of us like running in the heat, thus a summer marathon isn't a bad thing. The point is to make this decision with eyes wide open.

Lastly, let me say that none of these are show stoppers. Anyone can run a marathon training three days per week. My point is, help yourself to get the best advantage to enjoy the process and have a great, life-changing race. You won't be sorry.

CHAPTER 4
ESTIMATED RACE FINISH TIME

The tables are a guideline to predict what an athlete is capable of running based on previous results in a different distance. So, for example, someone who has run a 30:00 finish in a 5k race should be capable of running a 1:02:24 10k, 2:18:14 half marathon, and a 4:53:22 marathon. This by no means says that if they run a 30:00 5k they will run a 4:53:22 marathon. It is an indicator that predicts that it is possible, given proper training and enough preparation. There are many such predictors available on the internet, however, the one that I have developed takes a less linear approach with the calculation. I don't believe it is as simple as taking a single factor and plugging it in to get an accurate prediction. Longer races get proportionately harder to maintain pace. That said, this table has proven to be accurate with the athlete's I've coached over the years. If nothing else, it can act as a guide to see if an athlete is in the right ballpark with regard to their target finish time.

The table shows the pace, both in min/mile and min/km. Just keep in mind that the paces are based on running exactly 26.2 miles (42.195km), but running the blue line in a marathon is nearly impossible due to runner congestion, poorly marked roads or lack of focus. Running the line means running the course over the exact 26.2-mile line that the course was measured on. In some of the bigger events, this is actually painted on the road and it is easier to follow. Keep that in mind and shave a few seconds off per mile (km) in order to ensure you hit your targets.

Race Finish Time Predictor

5K	10K	1/2 Marathon	Marathon	Marathon Pace Min/Mile	Marathon Pace Min/KM
16:00	33:36	1:15:08	2:39:28	6:05	3:47
16:30	34:39	1:17:29	2:44:27	6:17	3:54
17:00	35:42	1:19:50	2:49:26	6:28	4:01
17:30	36:45	1:22:11	2:54:25	6:39	4:08
18:00	37:48	1:24:32	2:59:24	6:51	4:15
18:30	38:29	1:25:15	3:00:54	6:54	4:17
19:00	39:31	1:27:33	3:05:48	7:05	4:24
19:30	40:34	1:29:51	3:10:41	7:17	4:31
20:00	41:36	1:32:09	3:15:34	7:28	4:38
20:30	42:38	1:34:27	3:20:28	7:39	4:45
21:00	43:41	1:36:46	3:25:21	7:50	4:52
21:30	44:43	1:39:04	3:30:15	8:01	4:59
22:00	45:46	1:41:22	3:35:08	8:13	5:06
22:30	46:48	1:43:40	3:40:01	8:24	5:13
23:00	47:50	1:45:59	3:44:55	8:35	5:20
23:30	48:53	1:48:17	3:49:48	8:46	5:27
24:00	49:55	1:50:35	3:54:41	8:57	5:34
24:30	50:58	1:52:53	3:59:35	9:09	5:41
25:00	52:00	1:55:12	4:04:28	9:20	5:48
25:30	53:02	1:57:30	4:09:21	9:31	5:55
26:00	54:05	1:59:48	4:14:15	9:42	6:02
26:30	55:07	2:02:06	4:19:08	9:53	6:08
27:00	56:10	2:04:24	4:24:02	10:05	6:15
27:30	57:12	2:06:43	4:28:55	10:16	6:22
28:00	58:14	2:09:01	4:33:48	10:27	6:29

Fig. 1: Race Finish Time Predictor Table 1

Race Finish Time Predictor

5K	10K	1/2 Marathon	Marathon	Marathon Pace Min/Mile	Marathon Pace Min/KM
28:30	59:17	2:11:19	4:38:42	10:38	6:36
29:00	1:00:19	2:13:37	4:43:35	10:49	6:43
29:30	1:01:22	2:15:56	4:48:28	11:01	6:50
30:00	1:02:24	2:18:14	4:53:22	11:12	6:57
30:30	1:03:26	2:20:32	4:58:15	11:23	7:04
31:00	1:04:29	2:22:50	5:03:08	11:34	7:11
31:30	1:05:31	2:25:09	5:08:02	11:45	7:18
32:00	1:06:34	2:27:27	5:12:55	11:57	7:25
32:30	1:07:36	2:29:45	5:17:49	12:08	7:32
33:00	1:08:38	2:32:03	5:22:42	12:19	7:39
33:30	1:09:41	2:34:21	5:27:35	12:30	7:46
34:00	1:10:43	2:36:40	5:32:29	12:41	7:53
34:30	1:11:46	2:38:58	5:37:22	12:53	8:00
35:00	1:12:48	2:41:16	5:42:15	13:04	8:07
35:30	1:13:50	2:43:34	5:47:09	13:15	8:14
36:00	1:14:53	2:45:53	5:52:02	13:26	8:21
36:30	1:15:55	2:48:11	5:56:55	13:37	8:28
37:00	1:16:58	2:50:29	6:01:49	13:49	8:34
37:30	1:18:00	2:52:47	6:06:42	14:00	8:41
38:00	1:19:02	2:55:06	6:11:36	14:11	8:48
38:30	1:20:05	2:57:24	6:16:29	14:22	8:55
39:00	1:21:07	2:59:42	6:21:22	14:33	9:02
39:30	1:22:10	3:02:00	6:26:16	14:45	9:09
40:00	1:23:12	3:04:18	6:31:09	14:56	9:16

Fig. 2: Race Finish Time Predictor Table 2

CHAPTER 5
RUNNING SHOES & GEAR

One of the first decisions to make is what running shoes will you take with you on this quest. The choices are endless but that doesn't mean that they are all the correct shoes for you. Ideally, everyone would have the opportunity to go to a professional and have their gait analysis done. This would point the new marathoner in the right direction. Unfortunately, not only do we not all have this available to us, but, even when we do, what comes out of it doesn't always give us the best option.

Personally, I believe the only true way to find the right running shoe that suits us as an individual is to try them out. Run some miles in them and see how they feel. Even then, as they start to wear, the fit will change and your footfall will feel different. If you've been running for a while, you will probably have a good idea what shoes are the best fit for you in your training, but are they the best marathon shoes? That is to be seen. I suggest that if you are in the market for new trainers, ask around and see if you can possibly borrow a pair from someone your size. Especially if they enjoy running in them and find them comfortable. Try before you buy.

When it comes to sizing, endurance runners often find that buying a half size larger than the size worn for everyday shoes can be a good option. This is not always the case, but oftentimes it makes sense. As you clock up the miles on the road your feet will have a tendency to swell. It can be a good idea to have a little extra room in the toe-box to allow for this and still run comfortably. It won't necessarily prevent the loss of the odd toenail, but it can help prevent discomfort on the road. This is something that will need to be tried and tested.

Let's assume you had a gait analysis done; chances are that will give you some good ideas and your consultant will often offer an opinion as well. You can start there, but don't abandon what you have been wearing. When training for a marathon, it is a good practice to have a rotation of shoes that you can swap in and out depending on the type of run, the distance, and terrain you will be running on that particular day. By rotating shoes over the 20 weeks, you will reduce the risk of overuse injuries as each shoe will have its own landing profile and your footfall will be slightly different in them. My recommendation is to have at least two, but as many as is practical for you. There are runners who have dozens of pairs of running shoes in their rotation, (you know who you are). There is definitely a time for retiring an old pair, but it is worth starting out by reducing the amount of running you do in them and gradually taking them out of the mix as you work in newer pairs. If you have decided on your race day shoes, use these sparingly, maybe only for your faster runs and one or two of your long runs. When you feel good and confident in your race day shoes, you will run good and confident.

For a new marathon runner, be aware that you don't have to buy the $300 trainers. A good $50 will probably do the same job for you. My advice on this is to buy the best pair that is reasonably affordable for you. The expensive carbon-plated shoes are technically amazing and will help most runners achieve a slightly faster time. However, running shoes don't make the runner. If your goal is to complete the marathon and enjoy the experience then save some money and buy a comfortable running shoe without breaking the bank. When you complete this first marathon, you may consider splashing out on some *super-shoes*, but for now, it won't be necessary.

If, on the other hand, the *super-shoes* are in your budget, you may find that your feet feel more comfortable towards the end of the 26.2 miles than a shoe with less advanced foam cushioning. However, it's just as likely that less expensive shoes will suit you better. Having less expensive shoes will certainly not ruin your experience. That will come down to your preparation, and we won't leave that to chance. Another thing to keep in mind is that the new generation of carbon plated super shoes won't make a slow runner fast. They do give a runner who is running with sufficient power a little return on their foot strike, but, once again, the important thing is comfort over the long haul. The message is *find the right ones for you.*

There are many types of running shoes and depending on your needs you will need to decide which ones to get. If your marathon is a road race, and not being run on trails, then you won't need trail shoes. The caveat is if you plan to train on trails during your marathon training, then you may wish to include a pair of trail shoes in your rotation. Trail shoes generally have a thicker sole with larger lugs to help navigate stones, roots and other debris. They also tend to be waterproof without offering a breathable upper that is so much more comfortable when running over long distances. These are usually heavier and obviously not very efficient on the roads. So, unless yours is a trail marathon, these aren't going to be your race shoes come marathon morning. All that said, trail shoes as well as road shoes will come in the following options.

- Neutral/Cushioned shoes
- Stability
- Motion control

I would suggest that everyone starts with a cushioned/neutral shoe and see how that goes. I've seen it over and over where someone was told they need a support shoe, only to find that after a few weeks of training in them, they are picking up pain and injuries. It seems only logical to start with neutral and get support shoes if there are problems and you meet the criteria below for needing them.

If you can't find someone to do it or can't afford to get your gait analyzed, there are some at home tests you can do in order to get a better idea of which shoe may suit you better. However, let me stress that there is no better way to determine which shoes feel good on you, then by actually running in them. As a gait analysis may say you need a stability shoe, when covering long runs on a consistent basis, a cushioned shoe may actually feel better and produce less injuries. But let's first look at two tests you can perform on your own.

Test 1: Look at the wear pattern on some of your existing running shoes. If there is excessive wear on the inside of the shoes, you are likely overpronating. If there is a general wear in the middle or slightly on the outside of the shoes, then the type of shoe you have been wearing is probably the correct one. Keep using this type of shoe, especially if you are comfortable in them. One thing to keep in mind is that if you are wearing a stability shoe and there is wear on the outside, then consider moving to a neutral shoe as these shoes may be overcompensating for your particular gait. If it is a neutral shoe and the wear is on the outside, also continue with the neutral shoe.

Test 2: Place a piece of dry, brown cardboard on the floor and step in and out of the bath, shower, or even a bucket of water. Stand on the cardboard for a minute to allow for the water to be absorbed. When you step off again, analyze the footprint. A print that shows only a partial foot will usually indicate either a normal or high arch. A print that shows a complete footprint will indicate flat feet or low arches. This would point you towards a stability shoe while a partial print will indicate a neutral shoe.

A neutral/cushioned shoe, like the name implies, focuses

more on the cushioning and keeping the ride feeling more comfortable for a longer period of time. For marathon training and endurance running, this will more than likely be the best option for most people but it always depends on the individual. There have been some amazing advancements in the foam used in the newest cushioned super-shoes that, without question, provide a more comfortable ride over the course of a marathon. There are also scaled back versions that have just the advanced foam cushioning without the carbon plate. Honestly, there are so many options out there at the minute it is hard to keep up with the developments.

Motion Control shoes look to correct overpronation and are designed for runners who have overpronation issues caused by severely fallen arches. Overpronation is an exaggerated roll on the inside of the foot on each stride. This type of shoe is more rigid than stability shoes and therefore tends to be heavier. Motion control shoes are the opposite of neutral shoes on the extreme end of the spectrum and will be the least common of the three types.

Lastly, a stability shoe is designed for someone who has low arches in their feet which causes a less severe overpronation issue. A stability shoe will help keep the foot stable, limiting the inward roll. There are many different methods that each manufacturer may use, but at the end of the day, the goal is the same. It is supposed to help prevent common running injuries like plantar fasciitis, shin splints and knee pain. This is a middle ground between neutral/cushioned shoes and motion control shoes.

My personal opinion comes more from anecdotal

evidence and speaking to the hundreds of marathoners I've coached. That is to say, I've seen more people experience pain from switching to motion control and stability shoes, even when they've been told they overpronate. The more work done to change a runner's natural foot strike, I believe, the more chance of injury. Especially over the course of a relatively short 20-week training block where the goal is to complete a first marathon. As a runner continues to train for a few years, and finds improvements harder to come by, that is the time to fine tune things like that, but maybe not just yet.

RUNNING GEAR

When it comes to the rest of your running gear, make it simple and comfortable. When you line up at a big marathon event, you will see runners with a wide variety of attire. My advice is to travel as light as you can get away with. Anything that you have to carry or wear is another thing that has to travel the 26.2 miles, so choose it carefully. Some people choose to wear a bladder pack to carry their own water or electrolyte drink. These will also have pockets and straps for carrying gels and other food. Other runners might have a nutrition belt for carrying these things. Personally, I carry my gels in my hand and take the water that the race organizers provide. Most of the time this meets all of my requirements. All I will say is if you choose a device to carry these things, make sure you practice with it and it is comfortable.

There are also lightweight gel belts that can be used to

transport gels around your waist. Again, try these out well before race day. I have often seen runners with a dozen gels around their waist on the start line and moments after the starting gun goes off they are leaving a trail of full gels behind them as they become dislodged. A gel belt needs to accommodate your chosen gel packaging.

Hats, gloves, compression socks and sleeves should all be tried out and fit properly. There is some really good quality gear out there but, just like running shoes, price alone doesn't mean they will work for you.

If you are relying on headphones for music while running your marathon, then make sure the battery on your device can handle the time you anticipate being out on the course. These should also be very secure and comfortable. Secure, because if an ear-pod falls out on the course, the last thing you want to do is stop abruptly to pick it up. This could lead to a disastrous pile up of extremely angry marathoners. Comfortable, because these should be used for enjoyment, not causing pain and distress. Like everything else, try everything out on your long runs before implementing them on the day of the marathon.

Lastly, the night before your big race, make sure any battery operated device is fully charged and working properly. Don't just take it for granted.

LESSONS TO TAKE AWAY REGARDING SHOES & GEAR:

- If you can't get a gait analysis, try the at home tests

as a starting point to see what type of shoe may suit you best.
- Try a few different options and even borrow some from people you know who are the same size. Getting the right shoe for your training and your race is one of the keys to success.
- Consider buying a half size larger than you would for everyday shoes
- Keep old pairs and aim to have at least two pairs of trainers in your rotation and swap them out on your weekly runs.
- Use your race day shoes for some of your faster runs you will be doing and build confidence in them.
- Break in new running shoes slowly. Don't take them out of the box for your long run. Start with a 3-5 miler and gradually work them into your rotation.
- When it comes to other running gear, test everything before race day.
- Determine your strategy for bringing your gels or other nutrition around the marathon early in training.
- Make sure you charge your watch and any other electronic devices you will use.

CHAPTER 6
ADVICE AND WHAT I WISH SOMEONE TOLD ME BEFORE I FOUND OUT FOR MYSELF

Marathon running is a test of mental fortitude more than any other endeavor I can think of. OK, there are harder things in life, but very few that we will face willingly. As much as the idea of running a marathon sounds amazing, there are also plenty of physical challenges involved. As with most things, there have been methods for overcoming these that have been formulated over the years. However, unless you have the foresight to seek advice or coaching, you would have been in the same boat as I was when I started training for my first 26.2 miler. Here are some of the pointers I wish I had before I learned the lessons the hard way for myself.

STRETCHING

Imagine going on your first 15-mile training run. You are tired, extremely tired, and sore. But you managed it all the way without stopping. You jump in your car in order to go home, shower, eat, and put your feet up for the rest of the day. You arrive home, turn off the car and open the door. You realize that your legs just won't move. You want to swing them out of the car and onto the driveway, but they refuse to do as you ask. Lifting them seems like an almighty task so you incorporate your arms into the equation and make it a group effort. Together, your arms and legs along with an enormous amount of mental effort, you finally manage to extricate your legs from the vehicle. Nice.

Now what? Walking is excruciating. One foot in front of the other, slowly covering the 20 feet to the door and that much closer to the hot shower you desperately desire. Inch by incredibly difficult inch, you are covering the ground until finally your hand is on the door, (hopefully you didn't have any steps to climb). Halfway through the door you make the executive decision to skip the shower. You shuffle your way straight to the couch where you find the TV remote. The TV goes on and the channels are surfed mindlessly, looking for anything easy to watch while your pain slowly subsides over the course of a couple of hours.

In the meantime, you've been asking for someone to bring you food and drinks. All the food, and all the drinks. It is usually at this point that you question some of your life choices. "Was it worth it? Did I really have to do that? How the hell will I finish 26.2 of those miles? Shoot, how am I going to run 16 miles next Sunday?"

I'm not sure if this is how you are going to feel, but I certainly did. Here was my big mistake. I didn't stretch after my run. I simply finished my run and got into the car where my leg muscles seized up and refused to work again until I gave them some time off. However, if I had stretched, and given my legs a little more care at the end of the run, I would still have been somewhat tired and sore, but I wouldn't have been quite as bad.

When running for longer distances, leg muscles will tighten the longer they are in use. Performing a good static stretching routine, after a long run, helps aid the recovery process by increasing blood flow to the sore muscles and help stave off DOMS (delayed onset muscle soreness). Anyone who has gone to the gym and lifted weights for the first time in a long time knows the effects of DOMS. That's the feeling of stiff and sore muscles that makes someone walk like Frankenstein's monster. Not only does static stretching help immediately after the run, it helps in the days to follow.

Here is an example of some excellent stretches to perform after your run. The purpose of the static stretching will be to return your muscle to the length they were before your session. Each stretch should be held for at least 15 seconds to be most productive. A demonstration of each of these stretches can be viewed on my YouTube channel at https://youtube.com/@achieverunningclub

- 3 x Stand tall, reach for the sky, on your toes and hold for 15 seconds
- Spread legs shoulder width apart, fingers interlocked, bend at the hips, with your back

perpendicular to the ground, reach out in front - hold for 15 seconds
- Reach down intending to touch the ground - hold for 15 seconds
- Walk hands over to right ankle, put both hands around the right ankle – hold for 15 seconds
- Walk hands over to the left ankle, put both hands around the left ankle - hold for 15 seconds
- Slowly move back to the center and slowly raise up
- Put left foot in front of the right, dig both heels into the ground, lean forward on a bent knee - hold for 15 seconds
- Put right foot in front of the left, dig both heels into the ground, lean forward on a bent knee - hold for 15 seconds
- Stand on left leg and hold the right foot in your hand bent at the knee, keep both knees together, push your hips forward - hold for 15 seconds
- Stand on right leg and hold the left foot in your hand bent at the knee, keep both knees together, push your hips forward - hold for 15 seconds
- Hold left arm straight out in front, bring it across your front, pull in with back of right hand - hold for 15 seconds
- Hold right arm straight out in front, bring it across your front, pull in with back of left hand - hold for 15 seconds
- Big circles with arms moving forwards - 15 seconds

- Big circles with arms moving backwards - 15 seconds

As with each part of your sessions, this portion of your workout is important and should never be skipped. It will go a long way to help prevent injuries and reduce lingering soreness.

CHAFING

I'm running a 15 miler locally in preparation for my second marathon, this one coming up in Belfast. Training has been going well and I'm running my long slow distance runs at a gentle 10 minute per mile pace. This feels comfortable and I'm enjoying it. As it is coming into spring, the weather is a little warmer than it was during winter training. This means that I don't have a tight base layer under my t-shirt. What a feeling to be doing long runs in the warmer weather, quite a nice change.

The miles tick over nicely; 7, 8, 9, I'm well on my way around. I honestly don't notice anything out of the ordinary, other than I'm a little more sweaty than normal. As I finish my run, back at the house all I want to do is take a shower, put on some comfortable clothes and sit back to watch some mindless TV and eat something substantial. I make my way to the bathroom, get the shower started and find the right temperature for the water. I step in and turn my back to the steady stream of hot water cascading over me. Wow, does this feel great.

That's when I turned around and my life changed permanently. Holy cow! Who was stabbing my nipples with tiny little needles? The pain is otherworldly. I can honestly say that I've never experienced anything like it. Laugh all you want, but it was one of the most unpleasant showers I ever took. I never heard of nipple chafing before, but boy did I experience it. I mentioned it to my brother in passing later that night on a phone call. He said, "Oh yeah, I always put Band-aids on my nipples before a long run." The fact that nobody ever told me about this was a shocker. So, I'm here to warn you men, wear something over your nipples like adhesive bandages, a compression top or lubricate liberally with Vaseline or another petroleum jelly and that will prevent nipple chafing as you run longer distances. If you've been to any race, particularly one longer than 10k and during the summer, inevitably you would have seen at least one man, but likely more than one, cross the finish line with two streaks of blood down the front of his light-colored top. Like two bullet holes. This is someone who wasn't prepared for nipple chafing and someone who will be in agony later on in the shower. It is something you will not want to experience for yourself.

Women should be wearing a good sports bra, which should prevent chafing as a matter of course. However, nipples aren't the only place where we can chafe as runners. Thighs and under arms or anywhere that there is a steady movement of skin on skin or skin on abrasive clothing can all experience chafing. It is more likely to happen in the warmer weather when sweat is more prevalent, in the rain, when clothes get heavier, or when loose clothing is worn. The area can be sensitive for several days before your skin scabs over and creates a barrier to more pain.

    I actually had another opportunity to learn a lesson in chafing. I had an upcoming half marathon and my training was going well. I joined my local running club and was starting to feel like a *real runner*. Brimming with confidence a few days before my race I decided to go online and order a new pair of shorts. They arrived the day before the race and I was all excited to not only feel like a runner, but to start to look like one too.

    Race day rolls around and I wear my new shorts. The heavens opened while we waited on the start line giving all of us a good soaking. That's a fairly common assault for a runner in Ireland, and although it was unpleasant, it wasn't an entirely new experience for me. As I made my way halfway around the 13.1-mile course I started to notice my inner thighs sting, just a little at first. By mile 8, they were on fire. For the next 5 plus miles I ran like John Wayne after just disembarking from his horse after a long gallop through the desert. I was bowlegged and my pace had slowed down considerably.

    The lesson here was to never wear a new article of running gear on race day or on a long run. Anything new, whether a pair of running shoes or shorts should be tried out on a short run and gradually brought into your training program. This will give it a few times through the laundry and allow the fabric to soften and to ensure it fits you comfortably. It may not fit your particular body the way it does the models in the ads. Once again, it is a mistake that is usually only experienced once in a runner's career.

Another piece of advice is that if you have particular areas on your body that tend to chafe, consider applying petroleum jelly, or another lubricant, before your long runs. This is a common solution that many experienced runners advocate.

EATING BEFORE RACE DAY

I suffered a stroke in February 2017, at the age of 48, and that was followed up by heart surgery in November of the same year. It's a story for another book. As a matter of fact, I wrote a book all about it called A Heart for Running, and I'd recommend reading it as it is fascinating [shameless plug]. Needless to say, working my way back into decent running shape took time. I had resigned myself to never being the runner that I used to be. That is until I ran a 5k in County Cavan, Ireland and finished in 19:23. Not near a personal record, but it was one of the most emotional results I ever had. It filled me with confidence going forward. Maybe my fully repaired heart would help me become a better runner than I had been?

I trained hard in 2018 and into 2019 where I took my first shot at a sub-3-hour marathon finish in the MBNA Chester Marathon in October of that year. Everything was trending towards a really strong race and I headed into race day confident of a sub-3 result.

I traveled over to the Medieval English city and arrived the day before the race. We had reservations for an Italian restaurant for 8pm that evening. In 2019, I chose to eat pizza as my pre-race meal and this night was no different. We were a large group of 12 runners all looking to carb up for the run the next morning. By the time our food came it was 9pm, which is later than I normally like to eat and later than how I rehearsed it. The pizza was absolutely delicious, but maybe a bit too much oil and grease for a marathon runner eating his evening meal before the big event.

Early that next morning I met a friend for breakfast in the hotel restaurant where they had a continental breakfast laid out. We chose to have our own pre-packaged oatmeal porridge and some coffee. I also had two slices of toast and there were some croissants just sitting there, beckoning me. These looked like they may have been there for a few days, but thinking about the carb-requirement, I consumed one of these as well. Still feeling full of confidence, I headed back to my room to get my race gear on and finish off a few things, like going to the bathroom. This all seemed to go to plan alright.

I made it to the start line with plenty of time to spare and met up with 3 other friends all shooting to run under 3 hours. We stayed together, shoulder to shoulder, for the first 16 miles, bang on target for a 2:58 finish and keeping a steady pace. And then it hit me. I have never experienced bowel issues while running. I suppose I'm fortunate in that regard. But on this day, I suffered from mile 16 all the way to the finish line. I was almost doubled over with cramps the entire rest of the way. It came in waves. Wave after wave of stomach cramps for 10 miles.

When I did finally reach the finish line in 3:06:07, I headed straight for the portable toilets and spent the better part of 20 minutes in there relieving some of the worst cramp I've ever experienced. My sub-3-hour attempt was in ruins due to lack of planning and lack of discipline with my food consumption. I am sure this was caused by the greasy pizza and to a lesser extent by a stale croissant. Since that day, I've simplified my pre-race meal. I now eat a simple pasta and sauce with some garlic bread the night before. Breakfast is two slices of toast with peanut butter, 50-60g of porridge oats with fruit and honey, a large cup of coffee and a pint of water. I haven't had any problems since that time.

My advice in this regard is to test different evening meals every night before your long slow run in your training. Do the same for your breakfast before your long slow run. Rehearse what to eat and what time you eat. Start this process early in your program so that you have something that you are happy with before you reach the midway point and then hammer these details home every time you have a long run. Then, once you have both your evening meal and your breakfast decided upon, start planning for marathon day. If you have to travel and stay away the night before the race then start searching for restaurants that will serve up your evening meal as you like it. Make reservations for a time that allows for the food to be ordered, cooked, and served so that you can ensure you aren't doing anything different than you did in your training. Do the same routine for your breakfast the morning before the event, including the time you eat. Building a good morning routine early in your training block will make all the difference for fueling your run and getting your bathroom routine regular.

IN RACE FUELING

The first time I ran in the Dublin City Marathon, in 2013, I felt I was a seasoned marathon runner. More importantly, I thought at this point, going into my 4th marathon, I felt like I knew all there was to know about marathoning. Most of my new running friends were marathoners and we talked about running at every opportunity. We shared our experiences, as well as all the advice we read in books and online. I was full of confidence and my training had gone well. I felt strong and utterly ready for this race. I was making steady progress as a runner, with my times steadily coming down, so of course I knew it all, right? Wrong!

The Dublin City Marathon always falls in the last week of October, and for some reason, the weather is usually quite agreeable on race day and this morning was no different. This partly sunny and warm weather suited me down to the ground. The temperature at race time was between 60-63 degrees Fahrenheit, (15-17 degrees Celsius). Anyone that knows Irish weather will know that those temperatures feel warmer than they would in say a drier part of the world, so it was comfortable, and bordering on warm for many people.

In training I was taking two gels and we would usually plant bottles of water around the route we would take on our group long runs. So, in training, my nutrition and hydration were OK and I felt it would be OK for race day. I would take my two gels and water now and again at some of the water stops. What could go wrong? Well, as it turns out, lots can go wrong.

As we all do, I started out maybe a little faster than I wanted to, or at least faster than I had planned. Normally, this isn't a problem as we settle into a comfortable pace for the distance. Mile after mile tick over and before you know it, it is time for the first gel. I took mine at mile eight. It can be argued that this is too late. It can also, just as reasonably, be argued that this is too early. One way or the other, I took my first gel at mile eight and I felt excellent. I continued along, soaking up the amazing atmosphere in Ireland's biggest marathon, which just so happens to be the national championship race. This brings out the masses of supporters who watch some incredible athletes competing, as well as hordes of normal mortals, some running their first 26.2-mile race.

My body was starting to fatigue and I took my second, and final, gel around mile 14. Once again, I felt the benefit of the carbohydrates introduced, along with the shot of caffeine. This gave me the added energy I needed to get up one of the bigger hills on the course around mile 18. I hadn't been drinking much water at the stops. As a matter of fact, I took very little water as I felt it would slow me down and I didn't think I needed it. In my training, I had been stopping for water once along the route where we had planted bottles. I figured I could get away with one bottle of water over the course of the race.

After mile 18, things started to feel harder. Each step a little slower and more painful than the previous. I managed another couple of miles, but by mile 20, I was deep in the pain cave. So, is this what it's like to hit the wall? I didn't just hit it, I slammed into it face first. From mile 20 all the way to mile 26.2 it was a shuffle. I looked like, and felt like, I had aged 40 years over the course of 15 minutes. I'm not sure if it was the lack of water and I was dehydrated, or if it was the lack of fuel from only taking two gels, but it was agony. 6.2 miles of shuffling and scuffling and my pace dropped from an 8-minute mile to over 11.

It's a true statement, at least for the vast majority of marathon runners, that you will only ever hit the wall once. It's such an awful experience that you will address whatever was the issue and avoid it from ever happening again. I learned to fuel better and I take water, even only a little, at every water stop on a marathon course. Sometimes it is only two mouthfuls, but I always take some water. As for fueling, I now take up to 6 gels with me with the aim of taking 5 along the course, but always having one available in the closing 2 or 3 miles. This not only gives me an energy edge over what I used to do, but it is a psychological advantage to know I have something with me at crunch-time, from miles 23 to 26.2.

It is crucial to note that when it comes to fueling and hydration, it is important to take onboard carbs and water before you need them. If you get to that point that you have run out of energy, it is too late. You will suffer and feel the pain that is hitting the wall. You will read more about this in the Nutrition & Hydration section later on in this book. Let it be said that you get no "bonus points" for not eating or drinking either during your training runs or in your race.

JOHN MCDONNELL

ARRIVING TO THE STARTING LINE

On the morning of April 23, 2023, I woke early, as I normally do, but this was no ordinary day. It was the morning of the London Marathon. I had high hopes of a new personal record and my training had gone almost perfectly. I made plans to travel to the start with my daughter and two other runners. We were all in different starting waves with mine being the first to go off. We got away early and met up at the underground station which took us to the outskirts of the starting area in Greenwich Park. My start was wave 1 in the green starting area. I like to arrive in my starting area early to enable time to prepare my race clothes, put things that I don't need into my drop bag and to use the toilets provided if I need to. I parted ways with my travel companions as they were in the red starting area and started following the signs for the green start area with about 45 minutes until the starting gun.

    It seemed like hours crossing the park, following signs for the green area. It actually took a good 20 minutes to get close, but the elite women runners were just about to go and I needed to cross the street in order to get to my area. I was in full panic mode as the stewards wouldn't allow anyone to cross the street until the runners had passed. With about 10 minutes to spare, I finally arrived in the starting pen, removed my warm clothes that I had on, handed in my bag, and searched for a toilet as I needed a last-minute pee. The lines for the toilets were no lie, about 50 people deep and there was no way I was going to get to go. Each colored area has three waves so the folks in line must have been in later waves, which left in 15-minute intervals.

As soon as I handed in my drop bag, wave 1 was called to go to the staging area of the start line. I was going to have to hold it a little longer than I wanted to. The starting gun went off and I fell into a very good rhythm early on and although I wasn't bursting, I could have used a bathroom break. I had trained so hard over the previous months that I didn't want to lose any precious seconds. Therefore, I held it in for the entire 26.2 miles. When I crossed the finish line, collected my medal and goody bag, it was another 20 minutes before I made it to the toilets in the finish area. I was bursting at this point and finally relieved myself. I'm sure this isn't a healthy thing to be doing. The good news is that I did manage to run 2:56:44, however, it could have been a lot more comfortable.

The lesson here is that whatever time you think is too early to arrive at your starting area, aim to be there much earlier. Even the best organized races will have long queues for the toilets and you want to be comfortable when running your first marathon, or at least give yourself the best opportunity to be comfortable. Now, for a first marathon, I would highly suggest stopping along the course at one of the portable toilets if you need to relieve yourself, but the point is to be relaxed and ready when it comes time to start running.

PACING

Pacing is one of those areas of running a marathon that so many people miscalculate and end up having a painful day on the road. The first marathon should be an enjoyable experience, finished off with a triumphant and joyous last 100m as you cruise over the finish line. If pacing is considered during the training block, then it shouldn't be a problem, but all too often, it falls apart on race day.

Picture, if you will, a talented and fast 10k runner. Let's say someone who can run a 10k in under 40 minutes. They sign up for their first marathon. Experienced marathon runners advise this person to choose a target time that is well within their capabilities. This is important. It is important to *respect the distance* and know what it is like to run a 26.2-mile race. For this particular runner they will find the training hard, for sure. Going from a 10k runner to a marathoner requires a lot more miles on the roads. It requires more of a focus on rest and recovery. It requires a completely different diet and nutritional regime.

This runner chooses a goal time of, let's say 3:45 minutes. This is a very realistic time for a sub 40 10k runner, as a matter of fact, it seems easy. Let's look at the figures. A 39:59 10k means the runner ran an average pace of 6:26/mile for 6.2 miles. A 3:45 marathon requires a runner to run at an 8:35/mile pace. This will be extremely easy, correct? Well, yes, it should be comfortable. But a runner of this caliber won't feel comfortable running the long runs slowly. They will find that the target paces for the faster runs will be too slow. So, they will run faster in these sessions. When race day comes around, they will feel strong and, in their head, 3:45 will be a walk in the park.

So, this person arrives at the start line feeling great. The starting gun goes off and they get caught up in the rush where everyone goes out a little faster than they plan. But this person finds this faster pace, say 7:30 minute mile pace is comfortable so they stick with it. They work out in their head that 7:30 per mile works out to a 3:16 finish time. Well, that sounds much better than 3:45 and that pace is easy. They approach 10k, and think this is way too easy. They hit the halfway point and still they are feeling strong, so despite targeting a 3:45 finish, they decide this is easier than they thought and pick up the pace a little more, down to 7:00/mile. All of a sudden, they've hit mile 17 and start saying to themselves, "I should have gone out way faster than I did. I could have run sub-3 hours for this race. I feel so strong here and I've only got 9 miles to go." They continue at 7:00/mile.

Then mile 18 comes and their pace has slackened a bit, back up to 7:30/mile. By the time the 20 mile marker arrives the pace is getting slower and their legs are feeling the effort. The current pace goes up to 9:00/mile. Mile 21 hits and wow, this has got really hard and now they are walking. There are still 5.2 miles to go and they are walking. Even walking is hard. The last 5.2 miles takes an hour and 15 minutes of pure hell. What should have been a comfortable 3:45 finish time turned into an excruciating 4:02:00 finish.

This may sound unlikely, but I assure you, this happens more often than it should. The common saying is that *the marathon starts at mile 20* and it is true. If you don't respect the distance, this could turn into an awfully difficult learning experience and one that, depending on the individual, could put someone off running altogether. The moral of the story is to decide early what a successful marathon looks like, train for that result, and stick to the plan. It's a hard lesson, but entirely predictable. As a coach, I can almost always determine at the start who is going to fall into this trap, and who will stick to the plan and execute. Oftentimes, depending on how the training has gone, I may work with the athlete to re-evaluate and move the target towards a faster or slower finish time.

MISSED SESSIONS

In the years I've been running marathons, there has never been a single training block where I didn't miss at least one session. It happens all the time. Even when I ran my best times, there have been days missed. The best training block I ever had was in the winter/spring training for the London Marathon. During this block I missed two days. With only two missed sessions there was no concern about my fitness and I went on and ran my best. In this case both sessions were early on, within the first three weeks. One was an easy run; the other was my long slow distance run. Normally, the LSDR run is a key run, but it was early enough and I had already built a good base before starting the plan so I wasn't too worried.

Inevitably, there will be some days when you just can't squeeze your run into your day. For whatever reason. No matter what you do, it just isn't going to work out. For non-elite runners, this is normal. We have work, family commitments, travel, sick days, appointments, whatever it is, there are going to be days that running just doesn't fit into the plan. This is OK and won't have a detrimental effect on your training, unless it occurs too often.

The warning to heed here is to put the missed session behind you and move on. Don't think you have to make up for it by adding it on to the next run or squeeze it into a rest day. Each session in a well-planned program has its purpose. There are certain principles that need to be followed when crafting a marathon training program. By moving one session or adding it on to another, this dynamic is changed. If you aren't working with a coach who can advise the best way to restructure the plan, then it's best to just leave it undone.

There are two exceptions:

- Your long slow distance run when you have already missed one. In this case, if you know in advance that you won't be able to run on the day this is scheduled, move it to another day, preferably avoiding doing a speedy session the day before or after.
- A key speed session. As this is your first marathon, you won't have too many key speed sessions. However, there are a few, so keep your eyes open for these.

If your missed session doesn't fall into one of the two above scenarios, just skip it and continue with the schedule as it is. This is also the case if you miss even 3 or 4 days in a row.

Just pick up where you should be and do your best to not let that happen again. However, it is extremely important to not miss too many sessions. Even your short, easy runs have their purpose and there is a reason why they are on your plan. Whether it is to promote recovery, or build weekly volume, or possibly to condition your mind and body to run on tired legs, each workout has a goal in the mind of the coach who programmed the session. The point is don't skip a session if it is at all possible to get it done. Marathon running takes a certain type of mental toughness that requires a runner to run a session, even when they don't *feel* like running the session. Besides, too many missed sessions in a row will likely throw your training off and force you to adjust your goals.

INJURIES

You have committed to tackling this challenge of running your first marathon and are grasping it with both hands. That strength of mind is something that will carry you through the process and over the next 20 weeks. However, 20 weeks is a very long time to be training towards a goal race. There is a good possibility that you will experience, at worst, some sort of injury, but hopefully, nothing more than general soreness and discomfort.

There are two categories of runners who decide to take on their first marathon. The first category is those who aren't committed to the process. They probably didn't want to do it in the first place. Maybe they were talked into it and just don't see it as being possible. This is not you. You purchased this book, which shows a commitment and a desire to get this challenge done. You are in the second category. The ones who are determined and will accomplish this goal no matter what it takes.

Some athlete's taking on their first marathon may find their body has rejected the process, usually around the midpoint in a training plan. The increased volume and frequency of running is new and their body is having a hard time adjusting. Niggles turn into injuries. Injuries start wearing on their nerves and confidence. It is extremely frustrating. For those people in the first category, the non-committed, this is the excuse they were looking for in order to pull out of the process and resume their normal, non-marathon training life. For those in the latter category, they will often spend a small fortune going to doctors, physiotherapists, and anybody that has a voodoo doll and some pins, in order to get back to running.

For those in the second category, sometimes it is just best to sit back and let the body heal itself. There is no magic or voodoo that will help. The athlete needs to put their trust in their body, their fitness and the entire process they are going through. Easier said than done, for sure. But that's the reality. A doctor who is not tuned into sports injuries will likely advise the runner to simply stop running. Non-runners just don't understand a runner's mentality. Physiotherapists who work with sports related injuries tend to be best equipped to deal with a runner who has experienced a setback. They will usually offer advice about strengthening opposing muscles and muscles around the injury in order to help aid recovery.

This is particularly effective in preventing the injury from reoccurring.

Four, five, sometimes even six months is a long time to be in training for one event, particularly for us non-professional athletes. It is also a remarkably long time for a runner to be training for a specific goal and to remain completely injury free and healthy. Imagine hitting the halfway point in training and coming down with the flu or a chest infection. It could easily knock a runner back a week or two. Or worse, let's say there's a pulled or strained muscle that requires two to six weeks rest. It is extremely important to put things into perspective and stay positive. Think hard about your goal for this event and adjust if necessary.

As mentioned earlier, your first marathon should reasonably be about finishing the race and enjoying the experiences. If that is the case and you miss a block of time, prioritize and execute a new plan. First, prioritize what it takes to get back to health. This may be rest; it may be rehab; it may be stretching. Whatever it is, don't panic. Unless your injury is too close to the event, there will usually be a chance to make the adjustments and carry on.

As for execution, work your plan backwards from race day. The most important workout on your weekly calendar will be your long slow distance run. Here is an example of executing a revised plan:

Let's say you pulled a hamstring muscle in week 12 of your 20-week plan. It could take three weeks to heal and requires no running for those three weeks. Up to now, your weekly long slow distance run has brought you up to 17 miles. A few key principles will need to be adhered to. First, don't worry, there is plenty of time to get back to training. As a matter of fact, there will still be 6 weeks, a full month and a half, to get back on track. At this point, don't think you need to make up for this by doing more of something else. Let your body heal, rest and recover. Doing more gym work, or walking vigorously may just delay the healing process. By letting your body do what it needs to do, and it most certainly will, you will be much more likely to reach your goal. The body won't lose all the fitness you've gained in the previous 12 weeks in the course of the two weeks of non-running. Additionally, we tend to come back stronger once the rest of our muscles have the chance to make the gains from the previous training as well.

You miss weeks 12, 13 and 14 and you are able to return to running in week 15. That is 6 weeks until race day. So, work the distance of your long run back from race day.

- Week 20 - Race day 26.2 miles
- Week 19 - 22 miles
- Week 18 - 20 miles
- Week 17 - 18 miles
- Week 16 - 14 miles
- Week 15 - First long run back 8 miles

As you can see, you can get back to, and beyond, your pre-injury distance by week 17. Obviously, the first few runs back will be much shorter and week 15 may look like this:

- Monday - ½ mile easy
- Tuesday - 1 mile easy
- Wednesday - Rest Day
- Thursday - 3 miles easy
- Friday - 5 miles easy
- Saturday - Rest Day
- Sunday - 8 LSD

Then pick up your plan as normal, but change the distance of your long slow run each week to adjust for the missed time, bringing it up to the desired distance for your longest run. Under such a scenario, you miss the taper period, but a good light week on week 20 leading into the race will help you feel fresh on the start line.

Here is another example. Let's say you hit week 16 and you come down with the flu. You have reached 22 miles in your training to date. You miss a full week, which means you are healthy again and able to run again in the middle of week 17. In this case, just pick up as you were and don't try to make up for the lost sessions. You have all the hard work done already, so look after yourself, prioritize good rest and nutrition and come race day you will smash it.

The point is, there are often setbacks and if you really want this, then you can accomplish it. Oftentimes the negative mental strain that comes with time off due to injury is far worse than the injury itself. The most productive way to handle this is to stay positive. Work on the things you still need to work on that doesn't include running. Pay much closer attention to your diet. If you can incorporate some yoga without straining your injury then do that. Start working on your mental preparation which is also an integral aspect of marathon running.

When talking about injuries, it must be said that prevention is far better than cure. I talk about a lot of these things throughout the book and over the course of the plan. However, I'm going to reiterate some of these things here. Taking a short amount of time throughout your week to look after your body may prevent you from experiencing pain and missing significant amounts of training. Here is a list of the measures you should consider during the course of your marathon training:

- Stretching
- Yoga
- Strength Training
- Shoe Rotation
- Regular Sports Massage
- Foam Rolling
- Focus on good rest and recovery
- Focus on good nutrition and hydration

BE CAREFUL WHO YOU LISTEN TO

One of the best things about being part of the running community is the support and respect you receive from other runners. However, recently I joined quite a few social media groups just to see what other coaches and athletes are saying and advising marathon runners. I was shocked at the amount of bad advice being circulated. Let me start by saying that there is no magic pill. There is no shortcut. No single training session will get you to your goal. It takes desire, commitment and consistency. It seems like everyone on these groups and forums are looking to try anything that will give them that little edge. The sad truth is there is nothing, if you don't do the training, you will be caught out.

The same goes for nutrition, strength training, and mental focus. My best advice is to keep it simple. I can assure you that the best athletes in the world didn't get to where they are by taking salt tablets before a race. They didn't get there by doing an incredibly complicated interval session. They didn't get there by drinking pickle juice. They reached the top by putting in the work, committing to the process and being consistent with their training. It takes time and like anything else worth doing, it requires effort. That's not to say you shouldn't take the salt tablets before a hot marathon, do the interval session in training or drink the pickle juice. I'm just saying, although there is a time and place for these things, doing these things doesn't mean you can do less training.

The thing is that the folks spreading this information on social media are probably trying to be helpful. They probably read an article and tried some of these things themselves and possibly even got some benefit. I've seen influencers saying you only have to run up to 15 miles in training. Others say that you need to run 28 miles in training. I've also seen some of these running influencers preaching that you MUST run this particular, very complicated, interval session in your training in order to hit your goals. It can be very confusing, even for someone running for years. Keep things simple and you will find it easier to reach that finish line of your first marathon.

LESSONS TO TAKE AWAY:

- Stretch after you run
- Take measures to prevent chafing
- Never wear anything new in a race or on a long run. Gradually bring it into training on shorter runs a few times before race day.
- Plan a safe pre-race meal and rehearse eating that exact thing throughout your training block. Do the same with your breakfast before you run.
- Search for restaurants well ahead of time and make reservations that suit your routine.
- Take some water at every water stop, even if it is only a little. In warmer conditions, take more.
- Plan out your in-race fueling to ensure you are getting at least 100g of carbs per hour during the race.
- Don't wait too long to get water and carbohydrates into you. If you are very thirsty or hungry, it may be too late.
- Arrive at the start line early and give yourself the opportunity to be relaxed when the starting gun sounds.
- Respect the distance. Determine what success looks like and stick to the plan during the race.

- Don't try to make up for the odd missed session. Just carry on as if you didn't miss anything and pick up where you are.
- Don't skip a session simply because you don't feel like running it, they all have a purpose.
- If an injury crops up, don't panic. You may need to adjust your plan or even your race goal, but oftentimes, the race can still go on.
- Injury prevention is better than cure. Review the list of self-care that will help you stay strong and healthy.
- Don't believe everything you read online. Social media is full of people willing to put someone down, or worse, give bad advice online. If you have any questions regarding your marathon, contact me personally and I will respond as soon as I get an opportunity. Contact details are at the end of this book.

CHAPTER 7
A CASE STUDY IN OVERCOMING INJURY

Glenda is an athlete I have coached for some time. She has been progressing in her running and taking great pleasure in the process of improving her running ability. Race after race and session after session she was making strides and wanted to take on what many runners consider the ultimate challenge, her first marathon. Like most people who take this decision, there are always doubts in the back of the mind whether this is a good decision or not. Having completed a ¾ marathon the previous autumn, I knew she was prepared to tackle this challenge and worked with her through her training. Glenda always has a can-do attitude towards every run and workout she does, so I was not surprised by her work-ethic and enjoyment of the program.

All was going well until week 6 of the 16-week program. Running was becoming painful and it got to the point that she needed to stop, not able to continue moving forward without experiencing pain in her lower back and mid-section. This caused her quite a bit of distress and anxiety as she questioned her ability to run this spring marathon. Glenda visited one physio after another, even her local doctor to try to get to the bottom of the pain, but nothing was working. Week after week she missed her running and I dropped her running workload to zero, no running at all.

As the end of week 10 rolled around, feeling completely overwhelmed and defeated, Glenda went through the training log that we share and noticed in the days just before all the pain started, she had made some notes that struck a chord. She realized that this whole thing could be a kidney infection and decided to visit the doctor once again. He agreed and prescribed an antibiotic. Within a couple of days her pain was gone and she was fit to run once again. Unfortunately, it was now the beginning of week 11 and the marathon was only 6 weeks away and she missed a total of 6 weeks of good training and long runs.

We continued to adjust the plan and in the first week back, she did low mileage, running every other day. Given the time frame and her desire to see the job through to the end, and complete this race, we would need to get the ball rolling. The flights and hotel accommodation were booked and for the first time in a long time she had hope. In week 11, the target was a long slow distance run of 8 miles. In week 12 it was a 13 miler; we were having to ramp up quicker than I would have liked, but I was confident she could handle the volume. In week 13, the long run was 17 miles and Glenda was feeling great and her confidence was coming back. The bigger questions were coming; could she get to 20 miles and beyond?

With only three weeks to go, while many marathon runners start to taper, she was running her first 20-mile long slow distance run. She got through it with flying colors, but still had some trepidation about covering the marathon distance, so in week 15, we decided to do a 24 miler. This meant that there would be no taper for her first marathon. Her ultimate goal was to complete the marathon, feel great doing it, and time was not going to be a consideration. When the Sunday before the marathon came and she conquered that 24 mile long run, all her questions were answered. She was sure she could do it.

The following Sunday, Glenda and her family traveled to England to take on her first marathon and by mid-day she completed the course in a fabulous time of 4 hours and 47 minutes. This is sometimes what it takes. If Glenda didn't have that determination, it would have been easy to give up and say, "I can't do this now, I'm injured and missed too many miles." However, with grit and resilience the mission was accomplished and today she can call herself a marathoner.

CHAPTER 8
A REVIEW OF RUNNING TECHNIQUE & BEST PRACTICES

When running a marathon, you want to run as efficiently as possible. Anything you can do to make it easier to cover the distance will help make those last few miles a little more bearable. Here are some reminders for what good running form and technique look like. I'll also discuss pre-session dynamic warmups and post-session stretching. These two aspects of running will go a long way for looking after your body particularly on those days when you have a tough session or a long run.

RUNNING FORM & TECHNIQUE

For running, you want to run tall. This means you want to have a good upright posture. Follow these pointers below and work on them on each run. The easy run days offer a terrific opportunity to work on each of these points. Pick one or two and check in mindfully as you run and ensure you are running with good form.

- Pretend you have a balloon on a string tied to the base of your skull at the back of your neck, pulling you up from that point - Running Tall
- Shoulders should be relaxed and positioned back and down in relation to your torso
- Imagine you have a bowl of water between your hips and don't want to spill the water from the front or the back - maintaining a good upright posture
- Your arms should be at 90 degree angles and swing back and forth without crossing in front of your chest
- Your chest should be out forward, opening up your lungs to allow for easier breathing

When it comes to breathing, here are a few pointers that will help you get as much oxygen in as you go:

- Breathe through your mouth **and** your nose. This allows you to get as much oxygen as possible as quickly as possible. You will almost never see a runner, running at effort, with their mouth closed.
- Use a breathing pattern like two strides per breath in and three strides per breath out. This means that each time your foot hits the ground you take a partial breath in or out. There are a number of

- advantages to using a breathing technique like this, but for one thing, it reduces the chances of getting a stitch.
- Counting your cadence when you run is really useful. Your cadence is the number of times your feet hit the ground while you are running. It is measured in strides per minute. Counting your cadence while using a breathing pattern, like the one above, takes your mind off the discomfort you may be experiencing. It also gives you a good idea of your pace, much like a metronome would. It makes it much easier to know if you are going faster than normal or if your pace has slackened.

Now that I've covered the basic form and breathing techniques I am going to introduce a couple of new topics; uphill running and downhill running. Unless you have an unusually flat marathon, both of these are going to eventually be important to you when you run your race. Once again, there is no magic pill that makes running hills easy, but I can give you some coaching points to help you get up and down efficiently. When discussing running uphill and downhill I am making two assumptions. First of all, the hills you are doing are runnable. Some hills just aren't runnable. If they are too steep going up, you may need to put your hands on your thighs and do a power walk. Some hills are too steep going down and are dangerous to run down, particularly for those who haven't been running for years.

The second assumption is that we aren't racing for

personal records. Let's get up these hills and down the other side in one piece. When it comes to hills, you will find some hill sessions on the plan as well as some hilly runs. Try to use these techniques when running those sessions. The more you practice on hills, the better at running them you will be.

Uphill Running

This is one of the most intimidating aspects of running. Some runners report that their heart rate rises when just looking at an upcoming hill. There is no doubt that it takes more effort to go uphill than it does to go down or run on the flat. But here is one of the first key principles on our uphill running tuition; running by effort. Running uphill will be slower, but try to keep the same level of effort as you had before you reached the hill. You will have a downhill on the other side to make up for the lost time. Just work with the hill, slow down and maintain effort.

The natural tendency will be to lean into the hill, but this will work against you. Especially when leaning from the hips. A slight lean at the ankle joint will be beneficial, but a lean from the hips will make breathing a little bit harder and your center of gravity off balance. You want to be able to take in as much oxygen as possible. So remain running tall and keep your chest out and open.

The next thing to work on is shortening your stride. This will come naturally. It is easier to run with good form up a hill as the terrain encourages a shorter stride and a forefoot strike. You will instinctively be landing on your forefoot and recruiting your posterior chain muscles, (glutes, hamstrings and calves), to power up.

Next is to really drive your arms. Your arms should be bent at the elbow at a 90 degree angle. They should be driving straight forward and backward. Try to not cross your arms over in front of your chest as this closes the chest up and makes it a little harder to breathe. A good visual to keep in mind is to try to use your arms as if you are cross-country skiing and pushing yourself forward as your arm goes back. Another visual you may want to use is to drive your arm back as if you are trying to elbow someone directly behind you (we all want to do that now and again).

As your arms go, so go your legs. If you want to move your legs at a certain pace, you can begin by driving your arms at that pace. It is very difficult to move your arms and legs at a different speed. Try running at a slow pace and move your arms at a fast pace. See, it's very difficult.

When running uphill, your arms are vital to providing momentum. Drive your arms hard and your legs will follow. Keep your arm swing lower, trying not to increase the length of the swing. Rather, a shorter, quicker arm swing will promote shorter and quicker strides.

Uphill running pointers:

- Maintain effort, not speed
- Remain running tall
- Short, powerful arm drive
- Shorter strides
- Landing on your forefoot

Downhill Running

Running downhill certainly sounds a lot more fun than running uphill. I can assure you, 90% of the time this is the case. Keep in mind though, that not everyone runs downhill effectively. Some people who run well uphill, aren't great downhill runners and the opposite is sometimes true. Having good form and technique running downhill can make a massive difference.

When running downhill, there is more strain on your quadriceps as opposed to running uphill which strains your calves and hamstrings more. So don't be surprised when you start running hills, both up and down, when your legs start aching more. When going downhill, try to let the hill do some of the work for you. It is a great opportunity to get some recovery after going uphill and reaching the crest.

The first thing to do when reaching the top of the hill is reset your breathing. A big blow out and a big breath in. Maybe even two or three of these as you run and start your decline. Next, open up your stride. Longer strides will let the hill do the work for you. Gravity will pull you down the hill as you are in the air for longer. Longer strides will mean a slower leg turnover, and a slightly lower cadence. When you were going up the hill, you were taking shorter strides now you do the opposite.

The next key is to ensure you are well balanced. You may find it easier to hold your arms away from your body just a little to help maintain your balance, much like walking across a 2x4 or a balance beam.

Lastly, try to keep a slight bend in the knee on the leg as it lands. This will lessen the impact on your knees, which will be more important if you are running a lot of hills or if the grade is rather steep.

PRE-SESSION DYNAMICS

The dynamic exercises we will be doing will be used to get your relevant muscles warmed up and ready to work. I suggest these are done before your faster sessions, hill sessions, and hilly runs. A demonstration of these dynamic exercises can be viewed on https://youtube.com/@achieverunningclub.

- Running in place
- High Knees
- Heel Flicks
- Straight Leg Kicks
- A - Skips
- High Skips
- Lunges
- Side Lunges
- Squats

By all means, do them before every run if you wish, but they are essential prior to your harder sessions.

CHAPTER 9
PHYSICAL PREPARATION

Running a marathon, your first marathon, is more than putting one foot in front of the other for 26.2 miles. You are going from a normal human, to an epic human over the course of those 26.2 miles. To be completely honest, the race is the celebration. Having completed the training is the real transformation. After putting in the hard work, finishing the event is no longer in question, but rather the icing on the cake, and you earn the title of *marathoner*. Training to complete this distance requires conditioning your body in various ways to handle the demands of such a grueling endurance event. Being physically prepared requires a wide array of factors including aerobic conditioning and strength training, flexibility and mobility training, good nutrition and rest. Each of these disciplines are vital to completing the full distance and doing so without collapsing in a heap at the finish line.

AEROBIC CONDITIONING

So, what is aerobic conditioning? In this context, it is the process of training, in such a way, that improves the ability of your heart and lungs to pump blood around the body to fuel your muscles with oxygen and energy during activity. Additionally, it will improve your body's ability to clear metabolic waste, otherwise known as lactate. Lactate is the byproduct that is left behind from your muscles burning energy when performing exercise. Naturally, the more efficiently your body can do this, the better you can endure long distance running.

There are so many ways to improve aerobic conditioning and every social media influencer will tell you something different. Unlike many coaches, who tend to over complicate training sessions and cross-training sessions to appear that they have the one and only method, I like to keep things simple. First of all, when marathon training, most of your aerobic exercise should be running. Additionally, in order to help prevent overuse injuries and impact on your body, it is advisable to perform aerobic exercises that involve less impact on your joints, particularly the lower body. These include walking, hiking, cycling, spin classes, swimming, aerobics classes, HIIT workouts, and pretty much anything that gets the heart rate up for an extended period of time.

Swimming and cycling seem to be the two favorite methods of cross-training for many runners. The obvious reason is that both of these are less impactful than running and, therefore, can be done often without taking a negative toll on the running sessions. These are excellent and well worth considering as a source of cross-training.

STRENGTH TRAINING

Strength training is often overlooked by runners as they start out. However, it is essential for optimizing performance and reducing the risk of injury. A strong core and lower body muscles provide the stability and power needed to maintain good running form while covering long distances. Strength training for a runner does not mean you must go to the local gym and push heavy weights. As an endurance runner, the goal is strong and lean, not strong and bulky.

If you are someone who enjoys weight training, that's great. Incorporate 2 to 3 weightlifting sessions per week focusing on compound exercises that target multiple muscle groups. However, you can get the same benefit, as far as running conditioning goes, from performing a bodyweight routine consistently over the course of your training block. Either way, a little strength work will go a long way. Make sure to strike the balance between weight training and running. The ultimate goal, at least for now, is to run the full distance on race day.

I coach my athletes to incorporate a 20-minute bodyweight routine every weekday. It hits every key muscle group with a focus on core work. It goes like this:

- Push Ups
- Crunches

- Plank
- Squats
- Dead Bugs
- Bicycle Crunches
- Lunges
- Close Hands Push Ups

Do sets of these and cycle through until you hit 20 minutes. Maybe you start with sets of 10 repetitions and move on to the next one. If you aren't able to execute the push-ups, consider a modified push-up leaning against the wall or back of a couch. When it comes to the plank, start at 30 seconds and gradually go for longer over the course of a month. So, for example in the first 4 weeks the workout may look like the following:

Set 1	Set 2	Set 3	Set 4
10 Push Ups	10 Push Ups	10 Push Ups	10 Push Ups
10 Crunches	10 Crunches	10 Crunches	10 Crunches
30 Second Plank	30 Second Plank	30 Second Plank	30 Second Plank
10 Squats	10 Squats	10 Squats	10 Squats
10 Dead Bugs	10 Dead Bugs	10 Dead Bugs	10 Dead Bugs
10 Bicycle Crunches	10 Bicycle Crunches	10 Bicycle Crunches	10 Bicycle Crunches
10 Lunges	10 Lunges	10 Lunges	10 Lunges
10 Close Hands Push Ups	10 Close Hands Push Ups	10 Close Hands Push Ups	10 Close Hands Push Ups

Fig. 3: Beginning 20 Minute Bodyweight Routine

AFTER 4 WEEKS YOU MAY FEEL LIKE YOU ARE GETTING STRONGER and can increase the reps and it may look like 3 sets of 20 of each within the 20-minute workout:

Set 1	Set 2	Set 3
20 Push Ups	20 Push Ups	20 Push Ups
20 Crunches	20 Crunches	20 Crunches
45 Second Plank	45 Second Plank	45 Second Plank
20 Squats	20 Squats	20 Squats
20 Dead Bugs	20 Dead Bugs	20 Dead Bugs
20 Bicycle Crunches	20 Bicycle Crunches	20 Bicycle Crunches
20 Lunges	20 Lunges	20 Lunges
20 Close Hands Push Ups	20 Close Hands Push Ups	20 Close Hands Push Ups

Fig. 4: Intermediate 20 Minute Bodyweight Routine

Once again, you may be feeling stronger after 8 weeks and go up to 30 reps or 40 reps and only get 2 sets of each within the 20 minutes. The point is that you don't need to spend hours in the gym lifting heavy weights to get the benefits of strength training as a runner. Doing bodyweight exercises will help keep you strong and lean. If using the gym and weights, a good strategy is high reps, low weight.

A good strong core as well as lower body strength will improve speed, endurance and allow you to finish the race strong. One of the reasons that this is the case might not seem so obvious. As you are training and the miles are piling up, you will most likely be losing a few pounds of body weight. What you don't want to lose is lean muscle. Ideally, any weight loss should come in the form of fat loss. Maintaining existing muscle and building stronger muscle fibers is extremely important. But remember, you are an endurance runner, not a bodybuilder. Light, lean and strong will be a good target.

Your strong core will also aid in two other aspects of running that often get overlooked. Balance and coordination are neglected areas for many runners, but working on these two things are also beneficial. Think about it. By definition, running requires a person to only have at most one foot on the ground at any one time. Your body will subconsciously auto-adjust any balance issues with each stride. Therefore, if you can give your body the least amount of extra work during the course of a 26.2-mile run, the better it will perform. Coordination offers similar benefits. Both good balance and good coordination make maintaining good running form much easier over the distance. Solid running mechanics will ensure you cover the distance in the most efficient manner possible.

Try standing on one leg for a minute or two at a time. The more often you do this, the better you will become. A good practice is standing on one leg while brushing your teeth. This will give you roughly one minute in the morning and one minute in the evening at a minimum. Alternating the legs, morning and night, gives equal opportunity for each leg. Once this becomes a little easier, you may try closing your eyes while standing on one leg. This will add a new and more complicated dimension to the exercise.

HEART RATE (PULSE RATE)

Over the last 10 years there has been a lot of talk about heart rate (HR) training. This is where you perform workouts within a certain heart rate zone. These are based on your max HR. This is personal to the individual so my max HR will likely be different than yours. There are some general guides to use to calculate your own max HR. These seem to change frequently and there are quite a few formulas, each with its own twist on the number, but they are all in the same ballpark.

Traditionally, it was always 220 - age. So, for a 40-year-old, their max HR would be 180. However, the most popular calculation these days is 211 - (.64 x age). Using the same 40-year-old as an example the calculation would be 211 - (.64 x 40) = 185.4 rounded to 185.

The five heart rate zones are as follows:

Zone 1: Very Light - 50% - 60% of max HR

Zone 2 - Light - 60% - 70% of max HR

Zone 3 - Moderate - 70% - 80% of max HR

Zone 4 - Hard - 80% - 90% of max HR

Zone 5 - Max - 90% - 100% of max HR

For you, an endurance runner training for your first marathon, we will be doing the vast majority of our running in zones 1, 2, and 3. We will touch into zones 4 & 5, but not on a regular basis.

RESTING HEART RATE

Resting heart rate can be an excellent metric to track over the course of your training block. As your fitness improves you should see your resting heart rate gradually come down. Resting heart rate is calculated when you are sitting still. If you have a sports watch it will calculate this for you. It is not calculated during periods of sleep. If you do not have a sports watch with a heart rate monitor, simply sit still, find your pulse on your wrist or in your neck using two fingers. Then count the number of heartbeats over the course of 30 seconds and then double it. This is your current resting heart rate.

Don't be too concerned about this coming down day on day and week on week. Track it as a trend and see if it comes down. This is a volatile metric though, as so many things can affect it. Sleep, weight, hydration, nutrition, work load, stress and many more of life's day to day variables can and will change your resting heart rate. Measure it daily and take a weekly average and then track that to keep an eye on overall fitness.

SLEEP

Adaptation is the process that occurs in the body as a result of consistent training. These changes include improvements in cardiovascular function, muscle strength and endurance. Adaptation typically occurs over a period of several weeks to months of consistent training and exercise. During this time, the body undergoes a series of changes in response to the demands your training places upon it.

Sleep plays an important role in the adaptation process for runners. During sleep, the body undergoes a variety of physiological processes that are essential for physical recovery from exercise. One process that occurs during sleep is the release of growth hormone, which is essential for tissue repair and recovery. Sleep also plays a crucial role in the regulation of the immune system, hormone production and metabolism. Each of these are crucial for overall health and athletic performance.

Studies have shown that sleep deprivation can have a negative impact on athletic performance and recovery. On the other hand, getting enough high-quality sleep will improve athletic performance, reduce the risk of injury and promote a healthy lifestyle, both physically and mentally. Nothing has improved my running and overall quality of life quite as much as the excellent sleep habits I have developed.

Throughout your 20-week training program, you should be aiming to get as much good quality sleep as possible. Prioritize sleep over nights out, late night tv, and other activities that keep you from your bed. We all require different amounts of sleep to perform at our best, and you know your own body better than anyone. For most of us, this will mean between seven and nine hours of sleep per night. The best science at the minute suggests that we follow both a bedtime routine as well as a morning routine. The most basic concept is to try to get up at the same time every morning and follow some sort of routine. This is the case no matter what time you get to bed in the evening.

This concept will probably not work if you do shift-work or cannot follow a routine for one reason or another. In such a case, just ensure you prioritize sleep over any other activity when you should be sleeping.

For an evening routine, it is recommended that we switch off electronics a full hour before bed. That includes the tv, computers, video games, and phones. Then about 30 minutes before bed find a nice quiet place to sit in peace and quiet. Eventually, shut the lights out about 10 minutes before going to bed. Then when you are feeling drowsy, get into bed and sleep well for the night.

NUTRITION & HYDRATION

It should be obvious that how you fuel your body will either benefit or hinder your performance. Over the course of a 20-week marathon training cycle nutrition can have a tremendous impact on your race-day peak performance. As with everything involved in marathon training, there are several things to take into account when it comes to nutrition. It isn't always what you consume, but when you consume it that has an impact.

First and foremost, it must be noted that everybody has their own particular limitations when it comes to nutrition. Allergies, intolerances, and even tastes must be taken into account. We will go through the basics of the macronutrients in this section, but when it comes to specific foods, that will be up to the individual.

There are three macronutrients and each of these play a crucial role in running performance. Carbohydrates, protein and fats provide energy and support various physiological processes. It is important to understand the role each of these macronutrients has in your training.

CARBOHYDRATES

Carbohydrates, (carbs), are the primary fuel source for endurance runners. They are stored as glycogen in the muscles and liver and can be quickly accessed for energy while running. Consuming carbs before and during longer running sessions will help maintain blood glucose levels, delay fatigue and improve endurance performance. Therefore, consuming carbs before a run, particularly long runs, is essential to provide your body with the necessary fuel to sustain exercise. Carbs can also be consumed during longer runs, often in the form of gels, sports drinks or snacks to help maintain energy levels.

Depending on how much time there is, between the time carbs are consumed and the time the athlete runs, will determine the best type of carbohydrate to have. The further away from the run, the more a low GI carb will be of benefit because they take longer to break down. Examples of low GI carbs would be fruits and berries, vegetables and legumes, brown rice, wholemeal bread, dairy, soy milk, and whole grain pasta.

If exercise is to take place within 2 hours, then higher GI carbs would be more useful as they are more quickly turned to energy. Examples of these would be white bread, rice, potatoes, sweet potatoes, and breakfast cereals.

Carbohydrates should also be consumed after your exercise. When you complete your runs your body will have depleted its stores of energy. Muscles will be best able to replenish its glycogen stores within the first hour after exercise. It is a good practice to consume some carbohydrates soon after you run to help aid in recovery.

PROTEIN

Protein is important for repairing and building muscle tissue. When you run, your muscles are constantly working and, if training particularly hard, will experience micro-tears that need to be repaired, this is part of the adaptation process. Consuming protein after running will help to make these repairs and improve recovery. Runners often focus too much on carbs for fuel and neglect to consume enough protein on a daily basis. Protein is vital for all athletes, and even more so as we get older. It helps us get stronger and faster than we were before our hard training sessions.

Protein should be consumed as soon as possible after your hard running sessions, whether it is a speed workout, hill session, or long-distance endurance run. It is recommended that some protein is consumed within the first hour after exercise to get the most benefits. As a guide, take 20% of your body weight in pounds and consume that many grams of protein for the greatest effect as a recovery meal. For an athlete weighing 150 lbs., that would amount to 30g of protein as a post session recovery meal.

It should also be noted that protein should also be consumed throughout the day as part of a healthy diet, not just after exercise. This is especially true for athletes. Another guide for runners training for a marathon is to consume at least 75% of body weight, (pounds), in grams of protein. So, the daily consumption calculation for an athlete weighing 150 lbs. would be 150 multiplied by 0.75 which would be 112.5g. Obviously, this is a guide, but try to be within 10% of that either way.

If you are someone who tracks your food consumption, a good target would be to aim for between 25% - 30% of your daily calories should come from protein. In this way, you give your body the building blocks it needs as a marathon runner.

FATS

Fats also play an important role for an endurance athlete. They are stored in the body as tissue that can be accessed for energy during exercise when glycogen stores are depleted. Many ultra runners will adapt their bodies to consume fats as fuel for their events, with less emphasis on carbohydrates. For a marathon runner, this is inefficient because burning fat is a slower process than accessing glycogen. I'm sure there will be those who disagree with this, but in order to run a successful, enjoyable marathon, I suggest a carb-based fuel source.

Fats are necessary for the absorption and transportation of fat-soluble vitamins, like vitamins A, D, E and K. These examples of fat-soluble vitamins are essential in keeping an athlete healthy throughout the training process and through to the finish line. Vitamin A for the immune system, D for reduced injuries and increasing muscle strength, E for healthy immune and cardiovascular systems and K for strong bones and a strong cardiovascular system as well.

They are also essential for cell membrane function, nervous system function, and as an insulation and protection for organs and tissue. The message here is to not neglect fats. They have a bad reputation because they are so calorie rich, but they are essential for a healthy athlete. It is important to note that not all fats are created equal, and some types of fats are healthier than others. Unsaturated fats, such as those found in nuts, seeds, avocados and oily fish are examples of healthy fats that should be included as part of a balanced diet.

HYDRATION

The key to a good hydration strategy is to keep the body well hydrated every day. Get into the habit of drinking water starting with a glass when you wake up in the morning. The ideal amount of water consumption for an endurance athlete will depend on several factors. These include duration and intensity of exercise, environmental conditions and an individual's sweat rate. As a general guide, start with this formula. Take your body weight in pounds and divide it in half. Consume that number of ounces of water per day. Using our 150 lb. athlete as an example once again, they would try to consume 75 ounces (2.2 liters) of water on an average day. The roughly equivalent metric calculation is body weight in kg multiplied by 32 to give you the number of ml (the athlete at 68kg x 32 = 2.176 liters). This would need to be adjusted for someone whose sweat rate is higher, someone who lives in a hot climate, or someone who does a particularly strenuous job, or on a long run day.

Now that we have a guideline for daily water intake, let's look at during your training sessions. Dehydration will not only have detrimental effects on performance, but can be very dangerous for one's health. Dehydration tends to sneak up on an endurance athlete.

There are a few guidelines to follow here. In order to get a good idea of how much water you are sweating out, it's a good idea to weigh yourself before your training session. This will be your starting point. Depending on your exertion, you may require water while you are working out. When you finish, get back on the scale and that will give you an idea of how much water you lost during the session. The idea would be to drink 16 ounces (500ml) of water for every pound of body weight lost.

Another method for checking hydration levels is to do the pee test. Under normal circumstances when properly hydrated, one's urine should be pale yellow in color. The darker the color, the more you need to replenish your fluids. It should never get to the point of being a dark yellow or orange in color.

ELECTROLYTES

One last point to mention is the inclusion of electrolytes in your in-exercise hydration routine and in post-run rehydration. Electrolytes are important for endurance runners because they help regulate fluid balance, nerve function and muscle contractions. While running, the body loses electrolytes through sweat, which can lead to dehydration, muscle cramping, and a much-impaired performance. Therefore, it is important to replenish electrolytes during and after exercise.

The main electrolytes lost through sweat are sodium, potassium and magnesium. Sodium is the most important electrolyte to replace during exercise because it helps maintain fluid balance and prevents hyponatremia (low sodium levels). Potassium and magnesium are also important for muscle and nerve function.

To replenish these electrolytes, endurance runners should consume sports drinks or electrolyte tablets. Sports drinks typically contain a mixture of electrolytes and carbohydrates, which addresses three important issues; fluids, electrolytes and energy stores. After a long run or a hard session, where an athlete experiences sweat loss, these electrolytes can be replenished with foods high in these micronutrients such as bananas, spinach, avocados and nuts. Many athletes will also take a sports drink immediately after such a difficult session. Electrolytes can also be consumed in tablet form or in water dispersible effervescent tablets. Many sports nutrition companies sell these and are available online or in your local running or sporting goods store.

It is important to note that similar to hydration, electrolyte needs can vary widely depending on an individual's sweat rate, environmental conditions and exercise intensity. It is a good idea to test out any nutrition and hydration strategies long before race day. Ensure your race fueling suits your body and the timing is right. If you feel extremely thirsty or are experiencing muscle cramps, it may be too late to salvage your target time. Try to get the water, sports drinks and nutrition into you before you need it.

PREPARING NUTRITIONALLY FOR RACE DAY

You will want to prepare for race day early in your training when it comes to nutrition. I suggest doing a little research well before the event as to where you will eat your evening meal the night before. This is a key meal and it is not the time to try the bacon double cheeseburger if you've not trained by having it the night before a long run. If you are unfamiliar with the location of the race you are taking part in, do some searching on the internet for restaurant recommendations or look into the restaurant at the hotel you are staying in. Check menus to ensure that the foods you are eating prior to your training long runs are available to you. Practice eating this type of food, as close to the local menu as you can get.

When eating to prepare for your marathon you will want to rehearse what to eat the night before the big day. We've all heard the term *carb-loading*. Well, there is a saying that goes, "the more you carb-load, the more you need to carb-unload." You don't need to over eat a carbohydrate rich meal the night before your race or your long run. A good method of getting your carbs is to eat a carbohydrate focused meal, like pasta, pizza or a rice dish, but nothing too big or fatty and greasy or even too spicy. A conservative approach is advisable, after all it is only one meal. You can be as creative as you want in the days following the race. Personally, I go with plain pasta with sauce and some garlic bread. Work this out for yourself but some popular carb focused meals before a long run include:

- Pasta & Sauce with Garlic Bread
- Stir fry served over rice
- Pizza (exclude fatty oil and meats on top)
- Protein like chicken or fish with Sweet Potato and veg
- Baked potatoes with protein side

In addition to getting your food choice right, consider making a reservation early at your chosen restaurant the evening before your race. Not only does the right food matter, but the right time to eat matters. It doesn't have to be an exact science, but the closer to your routines you can get, the better and more comfortable you will find it come race day morning.

I recommend doing some research well in advance of your race. If you are traveling and staying away for the race, scout out online for restaurant recommendations and menus that will cater to your needs. If they accept reservations, try to make one for about a half hour before you wish to eat. Do this early as before any mid to large marathon there could be hundreds or thousands of runners looking to do the same thing. Italian restaurants tend to fill up fast.

GELS & IN RACE NUTRITION

As long as you follow a relatively well balanced and healthy diet, your body will have enough energy for roughly an hour of vigorous exercise. Our bodies store this energy in muscles and in the liver. As you expend your energy throughout the day it is important to replenish these stores. However, none of us can run a full marathon in 60 minutes, or just over that. Not even the fastest athletes in the world will have enough energy stores within their body to last the length of a marathon. Therefore, in order to avoid hitting the dreaded wall, you will need to take onboard some nutrition along the way.

Sports nutritionists have developed gels, gel blocks and drinks to serve this purpose. If you use these or are looking to start, then you will need to test a variety and find what works best for you and your gastric intestinal system without causing the kind of distress that I suffered in Chester. The good news is, the options are endless. Some athletes can take sports gels without any issues. Gels can have as much as 40g of carbohydrates each and have a combination of faster and slower released sugars.

Obviously, there are other options for on-course fueling. The key thing to do is to find what works best for you and your stomach. Some alternatives to gels, blocks and sports drinks include:

- Raisins
- Sugary candy (jelly beans or gummy bears for example)
- Fruit
- Granola bars
- Cereal bars

The possibilities are endless. Just remember that it is the carbs you are looking for. Snacks that are low in carbs but high in fats or protein aren't going to fuel you as well as carbs. These macro-nutrients take longer to convert to energy. Whatever you choose to top up your energy stores on race day needs to be rehearsed during your training. This is vital.

If you choose something that is too large to carry during your race, a banana or sandwich for example, be sure to recruit some help so that someone can meet you on the course to hand you your nutrition. Only the elites have special tables on which to put their on-course nutrition. Don't leave it to chance. This is such an important part of the race that you will need to plan it carefully. When you take your carbs will matter. Begin testing different gels or alternatives early on. By the time you reach week 10 in the training program, you should have a nutrition plan in place that you can test and perfect before week 20. Many runners will take one every 30-45 minutes. Others may take one every 5 or 6 miles. Find a strategy that works for you.

How do you manage to carry all of these gels or snacks? There are several options available to you. Gel belts are popular as are running vests, and shorts with pockets. I simply carry my gels in my hands as I go. It acts as a good reminder that as I make my way around the course, and my hands are lighter, I'm getting closer and closer to the finish line. Once again, find a method that you can work with.

CAFFEINE

Caffeine can help a runner perform better. Try it out and see for yourself. A good strong coffee before a run can make for improvements in your performance. Caffeine helps your focus, your performance and even recovery. For me, I always have strong coffee about two hours before a marathon. I take it that early as it can affect people in different ways. Coffee is well known to have a laxative effect. In addition to coffee, some of the gels I use during a race contain 100mg of caffeine in each one. I alternate between a caffeinated gel and non-caffeinated gel.

Once again, the most important factor in whether or not to use caffeine before or during your race is whether or not your body reacts well to it or not. Test it out well before race day. You should be trying these things out before every long run on your training plan.

ALCOHOL

Alcohol is never a performance enhancer. You will hear stories of people who ran their best 5k completely hung over. Wow, terrific, imagine how well they would have run if they weren't hungover. That said, during the course of your training program, alcohol in moderation won't set you back. It can be relaxing, however, my honest advice is to avoid it during your training. It is a small sacrifice and it goes back to the question, 'what are you willing to do to hit your goals?' How important is hitting this goal? If the answer is very important, then 20 weeks is a relatively short amount of time to avoid alcohol. You will be surprised how many additional positive side effects it can bring; improved sleep, better focus, more energy and better athletic performance among them.

CHAPTER 10
MENTAL PREPARATION

Running is one of the most mentally demanding sports. There is no way to get around the fact that we have to live with that little voice in our head telling us how hard things are and that we should probably stop. Marathon running takes this to another level. Someone who naturally has good mental toughness will be well suited to marathon running. However, you can build this skill during your training to help make things more achievable.

For one thing, stoicism goes a long way in distance running. Being mentally prepared for every situation is one aspect that will be of use. When we get into the Race Phase of the running plan, you will use visualization to help guide you through your marathon. You will visualize all the positives like the high fives on the course and the finish line euphoria. These positive visualizations will help motivate and incentivize you. However, it is also important to be prepared for those late miles, when the going gets tougher. Mentally rehearsing these hard moments and picturing how you will persevere makes the act of doing so easier. Pushing through these pain barriers mentally gives you the ammunition you need.

Understanding and accepting that you will need to do hard things is another aspect of the stoic's mindset that pays dividends. You need to make sacrifices and when you are prepared for that, nothing can stop you. This thought pattern gives a marathon runner the ability to remain disciplined and focussed throughout the months of training. There is a bigger picture to account for, the greater good. In this case it is the conquering of a goal, becoming something better than you were before, in an athletic sense, as well with self belief and confidence.

Additionally you will be working on your mantras, the positive messages you will repeat to yourself when you are facing difficulties on your long runs. I offer suggestions in the race plan as to what these might be, but you will probably want to come up with some of your own. Positive messaging isn't only necessary while running. It is also helpful to keep reminding yourself throughout the day that you are a strong runner. Reinforcing your physical training with mental exercises is where a good marathon program will make you a complete athlete, able to tackle any challenge.

Being mentally prepared for your marathon will make your experience not only more achievable, but entirely more enjoyable. I said it before and I'll repeat it, runners have a shared experience of being able to do hard things. It is what makes us special in a world of mediocrity. When it is all said and done, your newfound mental toughness will carry over to the rest of your life.

CHAPTER 11
A CASE STUDY IN OVERCOMING SELF-DOUBT

Pauline is a 57-year-old athlete who has been running for a few years. For her, running has been a method of staying fit and in-shape. In the winter, her daughter convinced Pauline to sign up and run her first marathon. Up until this point, her longest race ever had been the half-marathon distance. Getting talked into a marathon can sometimes be a dangerous endeavor, but the fact that it was her daughter, probably gave her some added motivation. Being able to run the same marathon as a family member is a special experience.

I worked with Pauline from the beginning. Working with first-time marathoners is a rewarding experience for me and something I enjoy immensely. I explained my training philosophy and how we would work together to complete this challenge.

From the start I could tell that Pauline questioned her ability to complete this distance and, ultimately, if this was a good decision for her. Part of my job as a coach is to provide reassurance and help athlete's find that self-belief they need to run the full 26.2 miles. Throughout the program, there were days that her muscles were sore. There were days when the long runs just felt too long. But week after week Pauline knocked out the training with persistence.

As the week's wore on, Pauline began to feel a little overwhelmed, particularly with the pain, soreness and mental fatigue of the long slow runs. Running these distances are hard and they require a great deal of mental toughness and she was feeling it. There were some days that the tears would come when thinking that there were longer runs in the upcoming weeks. Questions come to mind about one's ability to handle not only the distance, but whether or not after all of this work is it really going to be possible. My advice is, and always will be, that it can be hard, but infinitely worth it in the end. With the right mindset, almost anything is possible.

A first time marathoner will find that when they eventually get past those first few really long runs, the short and medium long runs tend to feel a little bit easier. As the weeks progress, there is a sense that it is going to be possible. By the time we get to the Race Phase of the plan, most runners are feeling like they just want to get this done and over with. The closer Pauline got to her first marathon Sunday, the more confident she felt. However, as the saying goes, "the marathon is a 20-mile warmup for a 6.2-mile race." When the night before race day finally rolled around, we talked about everything, came up with a solid race plan, and I was filled with confidence. My confidence was passed on to Pauline because we both knew she was both physically and mentally prepared to reach the finish line. The following morning Pauline managed the course and executed her race to perfection and finished her first marathon in 4 hours 53 minutes. The tears of pain and suffering in training transformed into tears of joy within seconds of crossing the line.

Most of us will have self-doubts when training for our first marathon. But with trust in yourself, your coach and your training, overcoming these doubts will transform you from an ordinary runner into an epic marathoner in only 26.2 miles.

CHAPTER 12
WHAT TO DO IN THE DAYS BEFORE THE MARATHON

In the final week leading up to your first marathon, there are so many things to think about and to be prepared for.

In this chapter I aim to give you some advice on how to best prepare yourself to ensure that your first marathon goes off without a hitch. The last thing you need is to be heading away in the day or two before the race and be unsure about what to expect. Every race is going to be slightly different, but most will send a race day preparation file, either by email or in the post. Be sure to read it and familiarize yourself with how and where you should arrive at the event to make it the least stressful as possible.

Additionally, before you get to the actual training plan, which comes next, I go through some of the race day preparations to consider as well as some decisions to make for when you run the marathon.

THE EXPO

If it is a big city marathon, you will likely have an expo to visit in order to pick up your race bib (number) and whatever the sponsors are giving out as token gifts. These are normally sports nutrition supplements, gels, reflective gear, and thousands of leaflets encouraging you to sign up for another big city marathon. By all means go and enjoy the expo, but make an effort to not put in 20,000 steps walking around the day before your big race. You trained too hard and too long to tire your legs out at the expo.

WALKING & TOURING

Once again, if you are running in a big city event, and especially if it is a city that you have never visited, avoid the trap of hitting all the tourist spots, until after your marathon. A hop-on, hop-off bus tour may be a good alternative to putting the miles on your legs. The best advice here is to plan ahead and keep in mind the little things that can make for a long day on your feet.

BAG DROP & THROW AWAYS

The drop bag is a bag that you fill with items you think you may need when you finish the race or things that you want to bring to the race but don't want while you are running. Think carefully about what you put in this bag. This may differ depending on the time of year that your race is taking place.

If the race is going off on a cold day, you may consider having the following items in your bag:

- A sweatshirt as your body temperature will drop when you finish the race and as it's cold out, you will need something warm to put on.
- Warm hat and gloves for the same reason as above
- A rain jacket will be useful in the case of rain. Again, your body temperature will drop when you finish and a cold rain will feel ten times worse after a marathon than on any other day.
- Some cash, (or a debit/credit card), just in case you need to get a hot or a cold drink after finishing. You just never know what you may need it for, but it won't take up much space and may just be exactly what you need.
- A mobile phone. Once again, just in case you need it to find people or directions in an unfamiliar city.
- Some snacks as you may feel like you need to replenish your calories soon after completion.
- A small bottle of water or a soft drink like a cola which would be good to replenish the sugars in your system.
- Pain killers may just come in handy as well.
- For a spring or summer marathon, depending on conditions you may want to include all or some of the above as well as some after sun or sunblock.

If the weather before your race is going to be cold, or even just slightly chilly, you should consider wearing something to the start line that you are willing to throw away or donate to charity. This can be rain gear, a sweatshirt or even just an empty trash bag. You just want to be warm right up until you start running. Many runners will make a visit to a local charity shop to purchase some warm start-line clothes that they plan on leaving behind. Most marathon organizers expect this and ask you to discard these items of clothing as you pass a certain point along the start. They, in turn will donate these to one of their local charities. It's a great way to benefit a charity on two fronts, with the purchase and the donation.

TO RUN WITH A PACER OR NOT

There are a few more decisions to make regarding your marathon. One of these things is, are you going to run with a pacer or not? For most first-time marathoners, I suggest going out and running your own race, at your own pace. Take the pressure of keeping up with a pacer, who will normally have a large group of runners with them all aiming for the same goal. However, this can greatly help someone looking for a target finish time. The fact that there is a big group running together may make it easier to push through the harder spells in the run. Pacers will also tend to be quite motivational and offer advice along the way. The risk is that you don't know how the pacer will actually run. Some pacers like to bank some early, faster miles, while others will aim to keep a steady pace the entire race. It is a gamble and a decision you will have to make on your own.

POST RACE MEETING POINT

Another decision, and fortunately a much easier one, is where you will meet up with your friends and family after the run. Make sure you know exactly where to go. Most races will have designated meeting points. If you are going to use one of these, visit the meeting point the day before so that you know how to get there after the race. I am guilty of poor planning regarding this point, and I will reluctantly admit, it didn't happen just once. Get this one sorted and you'll be glad you did. The last thing you want is to walk aimlessly for miles after completing the marathon. Your legs will hate you for years afterward.

RACE DAY PREPARATIONS

This is not the time to try anything new. The night before your race, ensure you have an effective plan for getting to the start line. Eat what you rehearsed as your pre-long run meal, when you like to eat it. Have everything you need for your bag drop. Pin your bib onto your running top before you go to bed. Lay out all your race gear. Get to bed early. It is not uncommon for first time marathoners to have trouble sleeping the night before the marathon. However, the saying goes, "it's not the night before that matters. It is the night before the night before." Don't worry too much about sleep, just get to bed early and get out of bed early.

Give yourself more time than you think you need to prepare on race day morning; a lot more time. Eat your breakfast as you practiced all along. Do your morning routine that you do before your long runs. Get your race gear on and add those last-minute items to your drop bag. Arrive at your starting pen with plenty of time to use the toilets provided. Keep in mind the lines will be very long at these, so if you have plenty of time, it won't be a problem waiting. More and more races are utilizing urinal blocks, for both men and women, so keep your eyes open for these as they may not be obvious, but the lines move much quicker than at the portable toilets.

THE RACE

You've arrived early, you handed in your drop bag and you are on the start line. Look around you. Say hi to a few of the other runners. There will probably be many other runners in your starting wave also running their first marathon. Soak it all in and wish everyone good luck. The sport of distance running is full of supportive people and welcoming to runners of all abilities. This is a good time to do some dynamic exercises and warm up your muscles. You may be used to going for a short, easy run as a warm up for shorter races. At the marathon, a few short, quick strides will help ease the tension and get your body ready to run.

When the gun sounds and everyone lurches forward, be

careful to not get carried away with the crowds and get into an uncomfortable pace. Stay within your target pace, whatever that may be. 26.2 miles will not be any easier if the first three or four miles go faster than you are prepared for. As a matter of fact, it could ensure a painful finish. Once again, stay relaxed. Enjoy the atmosphere. There will probably be spectators holding up humorous signs and kids holding out their hands for high-fives. High-five them. Tap the signs that say, "Tap here for power!". Enjoy this first marathon. Take it all in. This is unlike anything you have ever experienced. Lastly, smile as often as you can, especially towards the end of the race when you are tired and grumpy and sore. It actually helps. Use your mantras when the going gets tough. Count down the distance as you get closer and know that this day is your day. This is the day you join the 1% of people on the planet who have run a marathon. Congratulations.

THE TRAINING PLAN FOR FIRST MARATHON SUCCESS

THE TRAINING PLAN

This is a 20-week First Marathon training plan. This plan has been used by hundreds of runners competing in their first marathon and who finished it with an immense sense of accomplishment and self-confidence. What once seemed like an impossibility became a reality. This will be you as well. During these 20 weeks you will gradually build weekly volume as well as the distance of your long slow distance run (LSDR). These are the two big factors in completing your first 26.2-mile race. The focus will clearly be on endurance rather than speed. That said, there will be plenty of challenging sessions over the course of these months, where you will work on hitting your marathon target. The training should be fun, rewarding, and most importantly effective.

I developed my **BPR** training method for marathon training and have successfully used it with runners of all abilities. It is a flexible and straight-forward running philosophy. BPR stands for Base, Pace, Race. In the **B**ase phase we work on building strength, promoting consistency, adjusting to an increased number of training days per week, and starting to build weekly volume and the weekly long run distance. The **P**ace phase for this program will start in week 9 where you will have an increasing number of sessions with slightly pacier runs, including intervals, CoP workouts and progression runs. The final phase is the **R**ace phase. In this last portion of the program, we work on getting race ready, particularly the mental preparation becomes the focus. Nothing is left to chance and you arrive on the start line in peak condition.

If you have been running for some time and are starting at a point where you can complete a 10-mile long slow distance run, then you can skip the Base Loading Phase and go to week 5 and this program will be a total of 16 weeks. You will need to adjust your starting date to suit. However, many of you will be starting from a 5k or 10k distance. That is fine and the first 4 weeks will be used to get you up to the 10-mile distance. This will be what I call the Base Loading phase. You will be slowly increasing your running volume and training load in order to start week 5 at a level where you can complete the 10-mile LSDR (explained below):

Phase	Timeline	Focus
Base Loading Phase	Weeks 1-4	The Base Loading Phase is where you prepare to meet the starting point in the remainder of the plan. It is where we build up to a 10-mile Long Slow Distance Run. This is the time to work on starting good habits that will last the entire 20 weeks.
Base Building Phase	Weeks 5-8	The Base Building Phase is when the focus is building up the weekly volume and work on strength building sessions. This is also the time to start or maintain good habits, like drinking more water, adding appropriate protein to your daily intake and better sleep routines.
Pace Phase	Weeks 9-16	The Pace Phase is where you will start to see some more change of pace running and you will be introduced to some speedier sessions in general. Speed endurance is a key part of this phase as well.
Race Phase	Weeks 17-20	The Race Phase is all about race preparation. From mental training to tapering the running volume. The goal here is to be 100% ready for when the gun sounds on race day.

Fig. 5 - The BPR Phases of Marathon Training

This is much more than a training plan. It is a comprehensive program designed to get you to the start line in top physical and mental shape to complete such a monumental race. You will have transformed your running capabilities and cardio fitness possibly beyond where you've ever been before. You should have an understanding of sports nutrition and what your body responds well to. You will have excellent sleep habits and a healthy routine that will carry forward beyond your running life. The benefits of completing this plan cannot be overestimated.

During this program, I will take you through each week and explain what the weekly goal is and the reason behind each run. Over the course of these weeks and months the long runs will slowly get longer and the weekly mileage volume will increase. There will be cut-back weeks where your body will be taxed a little less and you will take the gains from the hard work you have put in. We will then start building once again.

As we move through the weeks, you will be introduced to a variety of different types of runs. Each time you have a new type of run, it will be highlighted in bold and the explanation will be found in the weekly notes as well as in the table displaying each session.

On the plan, there are four columns:

- The first column is the day of the week.
- The second column is the distance
- The third column is the type of run. If it is the first time this particular type of run is introduced it will be highlighted in **Bold**.
- The fourth column is the description and any specific instructions about the run for that day.

You will find a great benefit to your aerobic capacity if you perform non-running cross training like cycling, HIIT training, aerobic classes, swimming, or some other activity that raises your heart rate into zone 3, 70%-80% of your max heart rate. By cross training, you get the benefit of the aerobic workout without adding additional running volume, thus reducing injury risk.

It is important to appreciate that this is hard work. It is hard, but extremely rewarding. It takes discipline and commitment to the process. No matter what time of year you are training, you have to be willing to do what it takes. This includes running in the cold, rain, wind, and whatever else gets thrown in your direction. I always tell my athletes that skin is waterproof. Once you are wet, you aren't going to get any wetter, so keep on going. If it is snowy and icy outside, you may need to get on the treadmill at the gym, or put on the trail shoes and go off-road. Just commit to putting in the work. Before you know it, what once seemed impossible at the start will gradually become a reality. Where you once thought running 20 miles was beyond your reach, you will find it not only within your capabilities, but you will wonder why you ever doubted yourself as you crush your 26.2-mile race. As you enter the last two weeks of the program, you will be in your taper period. The goal here is to be in peak physical shape on race day. The months of discipline and long training runs will be rewarded with the most amazing and possibly life changing transformations you've ever experienced. You will be a marathoner, joining the 1% of the world's population who can say they have completed the marathon.

Most marathons take place on a Sunday. This is why the training week will start on a Monday and end on Sunday. It just lines up nicely for the typical event. That said, you can slide the training one way or the other to adjust to your schedule. Reminder: I suggest that if you miss a session or two, don't try to make up for it. Put it behind you and move on to where you should be in the plan. Each session has its own purpose and is situated on a strategic day during that particular week. If you miss more than a week, I suggest building in some easy miles and gradually building back to where you should be in the plan. The important thing to remember is that a missed session is a missed session. Don't think that if you miss an 8-mile steady run that you should then bolt that onto the back of the next day's 5-mile easy run.

Each week you will get a mix of training days which will include:

- Running sessions that will include one type of run or another. These will be described each day. Read these carefully as sometimes they may look the same as other runs, but can be slightly different.
- *No running* days. During these days, it is OK, and actually advisable, to cross train with some kind of aerobic activity like cycling, swimming, aerobic classes, or even going out for a walk.
- Rest days. A rest day should be a rest day, meaning no cross training. However, self-care like stretching,

yoga, and foam rolling are all advisable on these rest days. These are incredibly important for improvements and injury prevention.

THE BASE LOADING PHASE

For a first-time marathon runner, the ultimate goal will probably be to finish the race, feel good and enjoy the experience. You should have decided on your goal time and your target pace for the marathon, (you can use the race time predictor from Chapter 4 to help you determine a goal pace). You have a good shoe rotation of at least two pairs of running shoes as discussed in chapter 5. The Base Loading phase of the plan will focus on building up your strength and working on weekly volume and increasing your weekly long run. Begin building new good habits around drinking more water on a daily basis, aim for at least 2 liters of water per day.

WEEK 1

Focus: This first week is about establishing a routine. 20 weeks is a long time to train for a single event and one of the best methods of ensuring success is to build the habits that will keep you focused on the goal. During this first week you will be easing into the program, starting your journey to 26.2 miles (42.2k) and beginning the *Base Loading Phase* of the plan. You will start to develop a pattern and a habit of running 5 days per week. We have three different types of runs to introduce, the Easy Run, Steady Run and LSDR.

Weekly Volume: 17 miles (28k)

LSDR Distance: 5 miles (8k)

Easy Run: The Easy Run is executed at the easy end of the heart rate table, so ideally a zone 2 run. This is about 60%-70% of your max heart rate. If you aren't using your heart rate for training, we would call this a conversation paced run. You should be able to carry on a conversation without too much difficulty during this run.

Steady Run: The Steady Run is slightly pacier than the Easy Run and is run up into zone 3 – low zone 4 on the heart rate table, 70%-80% of max heart rate. If not using heart rate, then it is comfortably hard. You may not be able to carry on a conversation easily, but you should be able to talk in short sentences.

Long Slow Distance Run (LSDR): The LSDR is one of the most important runs on your plan. This one is a zone 1 – zone 2 run on the heart rate scale, about 50% - 60% of your max heart rate. These slow distance runs are key to building up the body's pathways delivering energy and oxygen to your muscles when you run. Run slow to run fast.

Additionally, we have a **no running day** and a rest day. A no running day is exactly what it says, don't run. However, you should do some kind of cross training whether it is cycling, swimming, aerobic classes, yoga, Pilates or even a walk.

A **rest day** is a rest day. Do nothing physically demanding. Perhaps some stretching or light yoga, but the goal on a rest day is to allow your body to make the gains from the hard work you are putting it through. Do not be tempted to run on a rest day. These days are equally as important as training days in your body's adaptation process.

Unlike the other session days, these no running and rest days can be swapped about for one another.

Week 1 Training Sessions - Total Volume: 17 miles (28k)

Day | Distance | Type of Run
Monday - 3 miles (5k) - **Easy Run**

Easy on the heart rate table so 60%-70% of max HR. This is a conversational pace and breathing should not be labored.

Tuesday - 3 miles (5k) - Easy Run

Easy on the heart rate table so 60%-70% of max HR. This is a conversational pace and breathing should not be labored.

Wednesday - No Running - N/A

No running days are perfect cross training days. Keep cross training relatively easy at this point in the training plan. If strength training, keep it at a level that won't impede your running ability in the days ahead.

Thursday - 3 miles (5k) - **Steady Run**

Steady runs are moderate on the heart rate table, 70%-80% of max HR. This should feel comfortably hard, but still able to speak a few words at a time.

Friday - Rest Day - N/A

A rest day means no running or cross training. These are perfect days for extra stretching, yoga, or foam rolling. Your body makes the gains from all the hard work while you rest which is why rest days are so important for making improvements.

Saturday - 3 miles (5k) - Easy Run

Easy on the heart rate table so 60%-70% of max HR. This is a conversational pace and breathing should not be labored.

Sunday - 5 miles (8k) - **LSDR**

The Long Slow Distance Run can be a zone 1 - zone 2 run, between 50%-70% max HR. This is the key run of the week and should be comfortable throughout. A great run to do alongside runners of similar ability.

WEEK 2

Focus: After a nice gentle week where you started to make some good habits and build a routine of running, we will continue along this path. Week 2, the second week of the Base Loading Phase, is similar to week 1, with a few extra miles (k's) and a Change of Pace (CoP) run. Once again, the objective of the week remains the same, building consistency and gradually building up your weekly miles and the distance on your weekly long run.

Once again, there is one No Running Day and one Rest Day. These Wednesday's and Friday's will remain consistent throughout the program. No running and rest days are just as important as your running workouts so make sure you take advantage of these.

Weekly Volume: 18 miles (30k)

LSDR Distance: 6 miles (10k)

The **Change of Pace** (CoP) run is sometimes called a tempo run or a fartlek run, but in this context, it is much like a combination of the two. You will start at an easy pace, somewhere in between 50%-70% of max heart rate. The middle section of the run is at a steady pace, 70%-80% of max heart rate. The last part of this run is back to an easy pace.

The CoP run will be a staple session in your program. It adds some zone 3 - zone 4 work and will really help increase your pace along with aerobic capacity.

WEEK 2 TRAINING SESSIONS - TOTAL VOLUME: 19 MILES (31K)

Day | Distance | Type of Run
Monday - 3 miles (5k) - Easy Run

Easy on the heart rate table so 60%-70% of max HR. This is a conversational pace and breathing should not be labored.

Tuesday - 4 miles (6k) - Easy Run

Easy on the heart rate table so 60%-70% of max HR. This is a conversational pace and breathing should not be labored.

Wednesday - No Running - N/A

No running days are perfect cross training days. Keep cross training relatively easy at this point in the training plan. If strength training, keep it at a level that won't impede your running ability in the days ahead.

Thursday - 3 miles (5k) - **CoP Run**

- 1 mile Easy (1.5k) +
- 1 mile Steady (2k) +
- 1 mile Easy (1.5k)

A Change of Pace run consists of an easy mile to start, followed by a mile at a slight change of pace faster and lastly 1 mile easy to finish it. The middle mile should be at a steady pace, a moderate heart rate, 70%-80% of max HR. This should feel comfortably hard, but still able to speak a few words at a time.

Friday - Rest Day - N/A

A rest day means no running or cross training. These are perfect days for extra stretching, yoga, or foam rolling. Your body makes the gains from all the hard work while you rest which is why rest days are so important for making improvements.

Saturday - 3 miles (5k) -Easy Run

Easy on the heart rate table so 60%-70% of max HR. This is a conversational pace and breathing should not be labored.

Sunday - 6 miles (10k) - LSDR

The Long Slow Distance Run can be a zone 1 - zone 2 run, between 50%-70% max HR. This is the key run of the week and should be comfortable throughout. A great run to do alongside runners of similar ability.

WEEK 3

Focus: You have been working hard in these first two weeks and building consistency. This is hugely important during this entire training block. There is no magic pill to get an athlete in marathon shape, it takes consistent, determined effort week-in, week-out. As the saying goes, there is no hiding in the sport of running. It is you against the road, so all the hard work now makes race day all that much more enjoyable.

This is week three of four in the Base Loading Phase. In addition to the Hilly Run, you will continue to increase the distance on your Long Slow Distance Run as well as your total weekly volume.

Weekly Volume: 21 miles (34k)

LSDR Distance: 8 miles (13k)

This week you are introduced to a **Hilly Run.** This is not to be confused with a hill repeat session. On a hilly run, you will choose an undulating route that runs over a few hills and should ideally include at least one challenging hill. Hill running has many benefits including:

- Building strength
- Helps build speed
- Excellent aerobic capacity workout

- Excellent for building mental strength
- Promotes good running form

WEEK 3 TRAINING SESSIONS - TOTAL VOLUME: 21 MILES (34K)

Day | Distance | Type of Run
Monday - 3 miles (5k) - Easy Run

Easy on the heart rate table so 60%-70% of max HR. This is a conversational pace and breathing should not be labored.

Tuesday - 4 miles (6k) - Steady Run

Steady runs are moderate on the heart rate table, 70%-80% of max HR. This should feel comfortably hard, but still able to speak a few words at a time.

Wednesday - No running - N/A

No running days are perfect cross training days. Keep cross training relatively easy at this point in the training plan. If strength training, keep it at a level that won't impede your running ability in the days ahead.

Thursday - 3 miles (5k) - **Hilly Run**

Choose an undulating route that includes at least one tough

hill in it. Hill training is a great all-around workout that trains strength, aerobic capacity, and endurance.

Friday - Rest Day - N/A

A rest day means no running or cross training. These are perfect days for extra stretching, yoga, or foam rolling. Your body makes the gains from all the hard work while you rest which is why rest days are so important for making improvements.

Saturday - 3 miles (5k) - Easy Run

Easy on the heart rate table so 60%-70% of max HR. This is a conversational pace and breathing should not be labored.

Sunday - 8 miles (13k) - LSDR

The Long Slow Distance Run can be a zone 1 - zone 2 run, between 50%-70% max HR. This is the key run of the week and should be comfortable throughout. A great run to do alongside runners of similar ability.

WEEK 4

Focus: This is the fourth and final week of the Base Loading phase. After this week you will be ready for the Base Building phase. The general routine has been similar for the past three weeks and it remains the same in week four as well.

During this week, you may start to feel the fatigue in your muscles and joints. It could be a very good time to book a sports massage. A good sports massage will often make those sore muscles and niggly knees feel as good as new in no time. Don't get me wrong, sports massage can be painful. However, if you prioritize muscle maintenance and injury prevention by getting one every 3-4 weeks, your body will not be sorry and you will likely not experience the pain from future massages.

Weekly Volume: 23 miles (37k)

LSDR Distance: 9 miles (14k)

You are introduced to a new type of run, the **Progression Run**. The Progression Run is where each mile (or km) is run slightly faster than the previous mile (or km). It is vitally important to get this right from the first mile (or km) as if you go out too fast then it will be harder and harder to increase the pace on each subsequent mile (or km).

WEEK 4 TRAINING SESSIONS - TOTAL VOLUME: 23 MILES (37K)

Day | Distance | Type of Run
Monday - 3 miles (5k) - Easy Run
Easy on the heart rate table so 60%-70% of max HR. This is a conversational pace and breathing should not be labored.

Tuesday - 5 miles (8k) - Easy Run

Easy on the heart rate table so 60%-70% of max HR. This is a conversational pace and breathing should not be labored.

Wednesday - No running - N/A

No running days are perfect cross training days. Keep cross training relatively easy at this point in the training plan. If strength training, keep it at a level that won't impede your running ability in the days ahead.

Thursday - 3 miles (5k) - **Progression Run**

The Progression Run is a classic workout and can be a lot of fun. The goal is to run each mile (km) slightly faster than the previous mile (km). I find it best to attempt to do this without looking at your pace on the watch, rather, run it by feel and effort. Running by feel will give you a much better understanding of pacing and effort.

Friday - Rest Day - N/A

A rest day means no running or cross training. These are perfect days for extra stretching, yoga, or foam rolling. Your body makes the gains from all the hard work while you rest which is why rest days are so important for making improvements.

Saturday - 3 miles (5k) - Easy Run
Easy on the heart rate table so 60%-70% of max HR. This is a conversational pace and breathing should not be labored.

Sunday - 9 miles (14k) - LSDR

The Long Slow Distance Run can be a zone 1 - zone 2 run, between 50%-70% max HR. This is the key run of the week and should be comfortable throughout. A great run to do alongside runners of similar ability.

THE BASE BUILDING PHASE

I n my book, <u>Marathon Training Strategies</u>, I explain that in the Base Building Phase we aim to build strength and stamina. This will get you to the fitness level that will allow for the more challenging workouts to be completed much more effectively. The initial Base Loading Phase got you to the 10 mile distance in your LSDR. In this second part of the Base Phase, you will continue to build strength and stamina by increasing weekly volume and the LSDR distance. You will see more hill training added into the program. Hills have a powerful effect for a runner. They are strength, speed and technique training in disguise.

In the previous phase, you started working on good habits. However, in the base building phase you should be laser focused on your nutrition, hydration, and sleeping habits. Some targets to be aiming for include:

- 2 liters of water every day
- At least 20% of you daily calories from protein sources
- At least 7 hours of sleep per night
- Executing every running session
- At least one additional cross-training session per week

You should be practicing your pre-race and race-day scenarios and have them nailed down by the end of this phase in week 10. This includes:

- Your pre-race evening meal decided on and practiced the night before each of your long runs
- Your pre-race breakfast meal decided on and practiced each morning before your long runs.
- Your pre-race morning routine in place and being practiced before each of your long runs.
- Your in-race nutrition plan in place and being practiced on your long runs

---

WEEK 5

Focus: From here on out we are into marathon specific training. This will be your first week of getting into the double figures for the long run. For many of you, this will be the longest you have ever run. Be proud of your accomplishments so far. Marathon training is a big deal and your commitment is commendable.

Weekly Volume: 25 miles (40k)

LSDR Distance: 10 miles (16k)

In week 5, you are introduced to **Hill Repeats**. Hill repeats are an excellent workout and will build strength, speed and aerobic capacity all in one. These should be run at anywhere between 75% - 95% of max heart rate, depending on the phase of the plan, but will touch into zone 5 if you are working hard. It is a good suggestion to take note of the location on your hill where you finish after the first 30 second interval. Then with each subsequent repeat try to get to that same place or further within the same time frame. Take note of using good form when powering up the hill and also when taking your recovery back down the hill.

Week 5 Training Sessions - Total Volume: 25 miles (40k)

Day | Distance | Type of Run

Monday - 3 miles (5k) - Easy Run

Easy on the heart rate table so 60%-70% of max HR. This is a conversational pace and breathing should not be labored.

Tuesday - 5 miles (8k) - Easy Run

Easy on the heart rate table so 60%-70% of max HR. This is a conversational pace and breathing should not be labored.

Wednesday - No running - N/A

No running days are perfect cross training days. Keep cross training relatively easy at this point in the training plan. If strength training, keep it at a level that won't impede your running ability in the days ahead.

Thursday - 4 miles (6k) - **Hill Repeats**

- 1 mile (1k) easy +
- 2 sets of 5 repeats x 30 seconds each uphill - slow downhill jog recovery
- 3 minutes static recovery between the two sets +
- 1 mile (1k) easy

Hill Repeats are exactly what they sound like. Find a challenging hill that will allow you to run hard uphill for at least 30 seconds. You should run your reps at 75% - 85% max HR up and when you reach your target time, 30 seconds in this case, turn around and do a slow jog recovery down the hill. When you reach the bottom, turn around and start again with no rest. When you finish the first set, take your allotted 3 minutes recovery at the bottom and catch your breath while standing still. Then do your next set.

Friday - Rest Day - N/A

A rest day means no running or cross training. These are perfect days for extra stretching, yoga, or foam rolling.

Saturday - 3 miles (5k) - Easy Run

Easy on the heart rate table so 60%-70% of max HR. This is a conversational pace and breathing should not be labored.

Sunday - 10 miles (16k) - LSDR

The Long Slow Distance Run can be a zone 1 - zone 2 run, between 50%-70% max HR. This is the key run of the week and should be comfortable throughout. A great run to do alongside runners of similar ability.

WEEK 6

Focus: Wow! You have already completed 5 full weeks of training and are one quarter of the way through your training for your first marathon. Give yourself some serious credit for this achievement. Staying consistent and dedicated to the process is so important and I'm sure you are feeling the benefit of the work so far.

As we work through the Base Building Phase, you will notice that for the first time so far, your weekly miles go above the total marathon distance. You will definitely be getting feedback from your running shoes by now and any other kit you will be looking to use on race day. If anything is rubbing the wrong way, causing blisters, hot-spots, or chafing then address it now while it is still early enough to find alternatives. If you haven't got yourself a sports massage, or at the very least, been foam rolling, then get started. The miles (km's) are building up and your muscles will need attention. The last thing you want is to neglect your body and find yourself missing time due to an injury. Prevention is always the best medicine.

Weekly Volume: 29 miles (47k)
LSDR Distance: 11 miles (18k)

Week 6 Training Sessions - Total Volume: 29 miles (47k)

Day | Distance | Type of Run
Monday - 3 miles (5k) - Easy Run

Easy on the heart rate table so 60%-70% of max HR. This is a conversational pace and breathing should not be labored.

Tuesday - 5 miles (8k) - CoP Run

- 1 mile Easy (1.5k) +
- 3 miles Steady (5k) +
- 1 mile Easy (1.5k)

A Change of Pace run consists of an easy mile to start, followed by a mile at a slight change of pace faster and lastly 1 mile easy to finish it. The middle mile should be at a steady pace, a moderate heart rate, 70%-80% of max HR. This should feel comfortably hard, but still able to speak a few words at a time.

Wednesday - No Running - N/A

No running days are perfect cross training days. Keep cross training relatively easy at this point in the training plan. If strength training, keep it at a level that won't impede your running ability in the days ahead.

Thursday - 4 miles (6k) - Easy Run

Easy on the heart rate table so 60%-70% of max HR. This is a conversational pace and breathing should not be labored.

Friday - 6 miles (10k) - Easy Run

Easy on the heart rate table so 60%-70% of max HR. This is a conversational pace and breathing should not be labored.

Saturday - Rest Day - N/A

A rest day means no running or cross training. These are perfect days for extra stretching, yoga, or foam rolling.

Sunday - 11 miles (18k) - LSDR

The Long Slow Distance Run can be a zone 1 - zone 2 run, between 50%-70% max HR. This is the key run of the week and should be comfortable throughout. A great run to do alongside runners of similar ability.

WEEK 7

Focus: This is the second to last week of the Base Building Phase of the plan. You are probably starting to feel the fatigue that comes part and parcel with marathon training. Make sure you have a strong focus on nutrition to help your body maintain and build the muscles you are challenging. Ensure you are getting a high proportion of your daily calories in the form of lean protein, whether they are meat or plant based. Consider supplementing with protein powder if you are finding it hard to get at least 20% of your daily calories from protein sources. As runners, this is traditionally an area of nutrition we neglect as it is widely felt that we need carbohydrates to give us energy on our runs. Although this is true, we also need a the protein to maintain and build our running muscles.

Weekly Volume 32 miles (52k)
LSDR Distance:13 miles (21k).

Week 7 Training Sessions - Total Volume: 32 miles (52k)

Day | Distance | Type of Run
Monday - 4 miles (6k) - Easy Run

Easy on the heart rate table so 60%-70% of max HR. This is a conversational pace and breathing should not be labored.

Tuesday - 6 miles (10k) - CoP Run

- 1.5 mile Easy (2.5k) +
- 3 miles Steady (5k) +
- 1.5 mile Easy (2.5k)

A Change of Pace run consists of an easy mile to start, followed by a mile at a slight change of pace faster and lastly 1 mile easy to finish it. The middle mile should be at a steady pace, a moderate heart rate, 70%-80% of max HR. This should feel comfortably hard, but still able to speak a few words at a time.

Wednesday - No Running - N/A

No running days are perfect cross training days. Keep cross training relatively easy at this point in the training plan. If strength training, keep it at a level that won't impede your running ability in the days ahead.

Thursday - 6 miles (10k) - Easy Run

Easy on the heart rate table so 60%-70% of max HR. This is a conversational pace and breathing should not be labored.

Friday - Rest Day - N/A

A rest day means no running or cross training. These are perfect days for extra stretching, yoga, or foam rolling.

Saturday - 3 miles (5k) - Hilly Run

Choose an undulating route that includes at least one tough hill in it. Hill training is a great all-around workout that trains strength, aerobic capacity, and endurance.

Sunday - 13 miles (21k) - LSDR

The Long Slow Distance Run can be a zone 1 - zone 2 run, between 50%-70% max HR. This is the key run of the week and should be comfortable throughout. A great run to do alongside runners of similar ability.

WEEK 8

Focus: Week 8 is slightly different with a longer Change of Pace run at 6 miles (10k). This should challenge you as you get your heart rate up for a longer period of time. Do your best to keep your pace steady for the middle 4 miles (6k). This week is a great time for your second sports massage. If you haven't already started, doing two to three yoga sessions per week will also be beneficial as you go on from here. Yoga provides some extra focus on stretching your sore and tight muscles. Mention to your instructor that you are marathon training and try to get some poses that target tight glutes, hips, quads, hamstrings, and calves.

This is the last week of the *Base Building Phase* before we transition to the *Pace Phase*.

Weekly Volume: 34 miles (54k)

LSDR Distance: 15 miles (24k).

Week 8 Training Sessions - Total Volume: 34 miles (54k)

Day | Distance | Type of Run

Monday - 4 miles (6k) - Easy Run

Easy on the heart rate table so 60%-70% of max HR. This is a conversational pace and breathing should not be labored.

Tuesday - 6 miles (10k) - CoP Run

- 1 mile Easy (2k) +
- 4 miles Steady (6k) +
- 1 mile Easy (2k)

A Change of Pace run consists of an easy mile to start, followed by a mile at a slight change of pace faster and lastly 1 mile easy to finish it. The middle mile should be at a steady pace, a moderate heart rate, 70%-80% of max HR. This should feel comfortably hard, but still able to speak a few words at a time.

Wednesday - No Running - N/A

No running days are perfect cross training days. Keep cross training relatively easy at this point in the training plan. If strength training, keep it at a level that won't impede your running ability in the days ahead.

Thursday - 4 miles (6k) - Easy Run

Easy on the heart rate table so 60%-70% of max HR. This is a conversational pace and breathing should not be labored.

Friday - Rest Day - N/A

A rest day means no running or cross training. These are perfect days for extra stretching, yoga, or foam rolling.

Saturday - 5 miles (8k) - Easy Run

Easy on the heart rate table so 60%-70% of max HR. This is a conversational pace and breathing should not be labored.

Sunday - 15 miles (24k) - LSDR

The Long Slow Distance Run can be a zone 1 - zone 2 run, between 50%-70% max HR. This is the key run of the week and should be comfortable throughout. A great run to do alongside runners of similar ability.

THE PACE PHASE

Training for pace is where things start to get a little more targeted. This phase is the longest phase of marathon training. In the case of a first marathon, it will last a total of 8 weeks. While we continue to work on strength, stability, balance and coordination, we now start to progressively work on pace. There are more weekly CoP runs and we mix in Yasso 800's, which you will learn about in Week 14. The focus is more to train athletes to hold the race pace for the full 26.2 miles and finish strong.

It is important to remember that in this phase, particularly towards the end of it, your body will be tired. Because of all the hard training, and despite the cutback weeks, you may struggle in some of the more difficult or longer runs. This should not be discouraging. This just proves that the plan is working. Ultimately, it is only after the next phase, the Race Phase, that you will begin to feel strong once again and, by race day, be in peak condition.

WEEK 9 (CUTBACK WEEK – YAY!)

Focus: Congratulations, you have been training for two full months. You have earned what I call a **cut back week**. This is where your body gets to have a lighter load and we *cut back* both the weekly volume and the distance for your long run. This is a very important week in the program. You need to let your muscles ease back now and again and catch up to all the hard work you have been putting them through. Everyone reacts differently to these cut back weeks, but whether you like them or not, they are necessary.

This is the first week in the *Pace Phase* of the plan. In my Marathon Training Strategies book, I define the Pace Phase as the part of the program that builds up your speed endurance. This is where we add more of a focus on pacier running. Most weeks, not all, will have two pacier runs each week. Speed endurance is vitally important for marathon runners because the distance requires a runner to maintain a pace for 26.2 miles. Even if your marathon goal is to finish the marathon, without a target finish time, speed endurance will be important. If this is the case and finishing is all that matters, then in your CoP runs and your progression runs, only change your pace faster by small amounts, but definitely try to pick it up a little.

Weekly Volume: 29 miles (47k)

LSDR Distance: 12 miles (19k)

But the *good* news is, just because the volume has been

dialed back slightly, doesn't mean the work is any easier. You still have a nice speedy workout in the mix. The last of the different types of runs you will see in this program are the **Yasso 800's.** These are one of the most common interval sessions for a marathon runner. The session was developed by Bart Yasso. He used it as a marathon finish time predictor. The theory is whatever time a runner can complete 10 x 800m repeats in, with a 400m recovery in between each one, will predict one's marathon finish time. For example, if a runner completes 10 x 800's at an average time of 3 minutes and 25 seconds each, that runner's predicted finish time in the marathon will be 3 hours and 25 minutes. It's just a matter of converting minutes and seconds to hours and minutes.

We will be doing a modified Yasso 800's session. In our session, we will be taking your goal marathon finish time and aim to complete the Yasso 800's using that time. So, if your goal marathon finish time is 4 hours and 30 minutes, then the goal would be to finish each 800m interval in 4 minutes and 30 seconds. So, we will be working it backwards. We will also not be doing 10 reps, so don't worry.

Week 9 Training Sessions - Total Volume: 29 miles (47k)

Day | Distance | Type of Run
Monday - 3 miles (5k) - Easy Run

Easy on the heart rate table so 60%-70% of max HR. This is a conversational pace and breathing should not be labored.

Tuesday - 5 miles (8k) - Yasso 800's

- 1 mile (1600m) easy +
- 6 reps x 800m with 400m walk/ slow jog recovery between reps +
- 1 mile (1600m) easy

This modified Yasso 800's session is an effective marathon-based interval session. The session consists of running 800m intervals. The pace to run these is calculated by taking the Goal Marathon Finish Time and converting it from hours and minutes to minutes and seconds, (see example at start of the chapter). Start the session with a 1-mile easy run warmup and finish it with a 1-mile easy cooldown.

Wednesday - No Running - N/A

No running days are perfect cross training days. Keep cross training relatively easy at this point in the training plan. If strength training, keep it at a level that won't impede your running ability in the days ahead.

Thursday - 6 miles (10k) - Progression Run

The Progression Run is a classic workout and can be a lot of fun. The goal is to run each mile (km) slightly faster than the previous mile (km). I find it best to attempt to do this without looking at your pace on the watch, rather, run it by feel and effort. Running by feel will give you a much better understanding of pacing and effort.

Friday - Rest Day - N/A

A rest day means no running or cross training. These are perfect days for extra stretching, yoga, or foam rolling.

Saturday - 3 miles (5k) - Easy Run

Easy on the heart rate table so 60%-70% of max HR. This is a conversational pace and breathing should not be labored.

Sunday - 12 miles (19k) - LSDR

The Long Slow Distance Run can be a zone 1 - zone 2 run, between 50%-70% max HR. This is the key run of the week and should be comfortable throughout. A great run to do alongside runners of similar ability.

———

WEEK 10

Focus: Week 10 is back to the hard work once again. At this point, you will start to see much more of the same type of training that you have been doing week in and week out.

Ideally, this is a great time for another sports massage. Whether you think you need it or not, it is recommended. So far you have covered 229 miles (370k). That is remarkable and just like a car, your body requires preventative maintenance.

It is a really good time to step back and evaluate your nutrition. Have you figured out how you are fueling your runs on your evening meal before your long runs? How about your breakfast before training? Have you tried gels or another source of calories during your long runs? It is best to get these things checked off by this point as you are in the middle week of the 20-week program and only 9 more long runs before race day.

You have two CoP runs this week. Hitting zone 3 and into zone 4 twice in the one week will add to your variability. When training for such a long period of time for a single race it is a good idea to mix things up. That is why you see different sessions each week. The CoP run is the most common session in this program, apart from the easy miles. As you get through these weeks and your fitness improves, you may find that your pace on the steady sections of these runs gets a little faster. However, don't be concerned if your pace isn't improving greatly. You have to remember that your body may be feeling tired. A really strong focus on good sleep should help you through the weeks with the bigger mileage volumes. Prioritize sleep over nights out, doom scrolling on social media or mindlessly sitting in front of the TV. There is only a short amount of time left before all this hard work and discipline comes to fruition.

Weekly Volume: 34 miles (54k)

LSDR Distance: 16 miles (26k)

Week 10 Training Sessions - Total Volume: 34 miles (54k)

Day | Distance | Type of Run
Monday - 4 miles (6k) - Easy Run

Easy on the heart rate table so 60%-70% of max HR. This is a conversational pace and breathing should not be labored.

Tuesday - 5 miles (8k) - CoP Run

- 1 mile Easy (1.5k) +
- 3 mile Steady (5k) +
- 1 mile Easy (1.5k)

A Change of Pace run consists of an easy mile to start, followed by a mile at a slight change of pace faster and lastly 1 mile easy to finish it. The middle mile should be at a steady pace, a moderate heart rate, 70%-80% of max HR. This should feel comfortably hard, but still able to speak a few words at a time.

Wednesday - No Running - N/A

No running days are perfect cross training days. Keep cross training relatively easy at this point in the training plan. If strength training, keep it at a level that won't impede your running ability in the days ahead.

Thursday - 5 miles (8k) - CoP Run

- 1 mile Easy (1.5k) +
- 3 mile Steady (5k) +
- 1 mile Easy (1.5k)

A Change of Pace run consists of an easy mile to start, followed by a mile at a slight change of pace faster and lastly 1 mile easy to finish it. The middle mile should be at a steady pace, a moderate heart rate, 70%-80% of max HR. This should feel comfortably hard, but still able to speak a few words at a time.

Friday - Rest Day - N/A

A rest day means no running or cross training. These are perfect days for extra stretching, yoga, or foam rolling.

Saturday - 4 miles (6k) - Easy Run

Easy on the heart rate table so 60%-70% of max HR. This is a conversational pace and breathing should not be labored.

Sunday - 16 miles (26k) LSDR

The Long Slow Distance Run can be a zone 1 - zone 2 run,

between 50%-70% max HR. This is the key run of the week and should be comfortable throughout. A great run to do alongside runners of similar ability.

WEEK 11

Focus: If you have purchased and downloaded the digital training log for use with this plan, available from https://achieverc.com/downloads/running-your-first-marathon-made-easy-training-log/, then perhaps you've been tracking your daily resting heart rate. This is an excellent metric to see how your fitness is improving. Ideally, your weekly average daily resting heart rate will be decreasing slightly week-on-week. That sounds like an oxymoron, weekly average daily resting heart rate, but this reading takes your average resting heart rate from each day and calculates the average of these figures over the course of the week. This is the number you should be looking at. If it seems to be trending upwards, then you may need to take an additional rest day here and there. Only do this in the case where the numbers are trending the wrong way and your body is physically telling you the same story. The only session that I would highly recommend not skipping is the Sunday Long Slow Distance Run.

This is not the time to get lazy though. If all is feeling OK, then this is the time to double-down on your hard work. Embrace the challenge that all this running is providing and stay the course. Remember the reason why you took on this marathon and let's get it done.

Weekly Volume: 36 miles (58k)
LSDR Distance: 17 miles (27k)

W__EEK__ 11 T__RAINING__ S__ESSIONS__ - T__OTAL__ V__OLUME:__ 36 __MILES__ (58__K__)

Day | Distance | Type of Run
Monday - 4 miles (6k) - Easy Run

Easy on the heart rate table so 60%-70% of max HR. This is a conversational pace and breathing should not be labored.

Tuesday - 6 miles (10k) - Hilly Run

Choose an undulating route that includes at least one tough hill in it. Hill training is a great all-around workout that trains strength, aerobic capacity, and endurance.

Wednesday - No Running - N/A

No running days are perfect cross training days. Keep cross training relatively easy at this point in the training plan. If strength training, keep it at a level that won't impede your running ability in the days ahead.

Thursday - 6 miles (10k) - CoP Run

- 1 mile Easy (2k) +
- 4 miles Steady (6k) +
- 1 mile Easy (2k)

A Change of Pace run consists of an easy mile to start, followed by a mile at a slight change of pace faster and lastly 1 mile easy to finish it. The middle mile should be at a steady pace, a moderate heart rate, 70%-80% of max HR. This should feel comfortably hard, but still able to speak a few words at a time.

Friday - Rest Day - N/A

A rest day means no running or cross training. These are perfect days for extra stretching, yoga, or foam rolling.

Saturday - 3 miles (5k) - Easy Run

Easy on the heart rate table so 60%-70% of max HR. This is a conversational pace and breathing should not be labored.

Sunday - 17 miles (27k) - LSDR

The Long Slow Distance Run can be a zone 1 - zone 2 run, between 50%-70% max HR. This is the key run of the week and should be comfortable throughout. A great run to do alongside runners of similar ability.

WEEK 12

Focus: Only one pacier session this week, so be sure to give it some effort on your Tuesday Progression Run.

If you have been doing any yoga or extra stretching sessions you will probably be appreciating it right about now. If you haven't, get started now. Your body will thank you for it and, although it may feel hard at the time, you will get immense satisfaction and a sense of relief from tight and sore muscles. So, break out that old, disused yoga mat and find some Yoga for Runners online. Or better yet, go to a nearby yoga studio and sign up.

Weekly Volume: 35 miles (56k)
LSDR Distance: 18 miles (29k)

Week 12 Training Sessions - Total Volume: 35 miles (56k)

Day | Distance | Type of Run
Monday - 3 miles (5k) - Easy Run

Easy on the heart rate table so 60%-70% of max HR. This is a conversational pace and breathing should not be labored.

Tuesday - 4 miles (6k) - Progression Run

The Progression Run is a classic workout and can be a lot of fun. The goal is to run each mile (km) slightly faster than the previous mile (km). I find it best to attempt to do this without looking at your pace on the watch, rather, run it by feel and effort. Running by feel will give you a much better understanding of pacing and effort.

Wednesday - No Running - N/A

No running days are perfect cross training days. Keep cross training relatively easy at this point in the training plan. If strength training, keep it at a level that won't impede your running ability in the days ahead.

Thursday - 6 miles (10k) - Easy Run

Easy on the heart rate table so 60%-70% of max HR. This is a conversational pace and breathing should not be labored.

Friday - Rest Day - N/A

A rest day means no running or cross training. These are perfect days for extra stretching, yoga, or foam rolling.

Saturday - 4 miles (6k) - Easy Run

Easy on the heart rate table so 60%-70% of max HR. This is a conversational pace and breathing should not be labored.

Sunday - 18 miles (29k) - LSDR

The Long Slow Distance Run can be a zone 1 - zone 2 run, between 50%-70% max HR. This is the key run of the week and should be comfortable throughout. A great run to do alongside runners of similar ability.

WEEK 13 (ANOTHER CUTBACK WEEK!)

Focus: You are doing amazing! Give yourself another pat on the back for reaching this point. You have completed three months of marathon training. This is another much needed cut back week. It is a good opportunity to work hard on your speedier sessions this week, and make sure to get plenty of good rest and relaxation with the reduced volume.

You will notice that in week 13 you have another hill repeats session. Look carefully and you will see that the number of sets, reps and your effort level are different from the last time you had a hill repeat session. Pay close attention and do your best to hit these targets. Once again, see if you can reach the same distance in each 30 second repeat (this will likely be further along up the hill from the last time you did this session).

Weekly Volume: 28 miles (45k)
LSDR Distance: 14 miles (23k)

WEEK 13 TRAINING SESSIONS - TOTAL VOLUME: 28 MILES (45K)

Day | Distance | Type of Run
Monday - 3 miles (5k) - Easy Run

Easy on the heart rate table so 60%-70% of max HR. This is a conversational pace and breathing should not be labored.

Tuesday - 4 miles (6k) - CoP Run

- 1 mile Easy (1k) +
- 2 miles Steady (4k) +
- 1 mile Easy (1k)

A Change of Pace run consists of an easy mile to start, followed by a mile at a slight change of pace faster and lastly 1 mile easy to finish it. The middle mile should be at a steady pace, a moderate heart rate, 70%-80% of max HR. This should feel comfortably hard, but still able to speak a few words at a time.

Wednesday - No Running - N/A

No running days are perfect cross training days. Keep cross training relatively easy at this point in the training plan. If strength training, keep it at a level that won't impede your running ability in the days ahead.

Thursday - 4 miles (6k) - Hill Repeats

- 1 mile easy +

- 3 sets of 4 hill repeats x 30 seconds each uphill - slow downhill jog recovery
- 3 minutes static recovery between each of the three sets +
- 1 mile easy

Hill Repeats are exactly what they sound like. Find a challenging hill that will allow you to run hard uphill for at least 30 seconds. You will run your reps at 85% - 95% max HR up and when you reach your target time, 30 seconds in this case, turn around and do a slow jog recovery down the hill. When you reach the bottom, turn around and start again with no rest. When you finish the first set, take your allotted recovery at the bottom and catch your breath. Then do your next set. And the same for the third set.

Friday - Rest Day - N/A

A rest day means no running or cross training. These are perfect days for extra stretching, yoga, or foam rolling.

Saturday - 3 miles (5k) - Easy Run

Easy on the heart rate table so 60%-70% of max HR. This is a conversational pace and breathing should not be labored.

Sunday - 14 miles (23k) - LSDR

The Long Slow Distance Run can be a zone 1 - zone 2 run,

between 50%-70% max HR. This is the key run of the week and should be comfortable throughout. A great run to do alongside runners of similar ability.

WEEK 14

Focus: In week 14 of your first marathon training plan, we are back to the harder work in this, the sixth week, of the Pace phase of your program. Only one speedier session during the week, this time on Thursday. The big run for the week is on your Sunday Long Slow Distance Run. This is the first 20 miler (32k) on the plan. If there was ever a confidence building run for a first-time marathoner, this one is certainly it. I suggest that anyone can run a marathon with the right mindset and this particular session goes a very long way, pardon the pun, towards creating the self-belief that long distance running requires.

It is very important to practice your in-race fueling and hydration strategy during this long run. It is also a good opportunity to practice a race day scenario by wearing what you intend on wearing during your big event. Make this one a dress rehearsal for marathon morning from your pre-run evening meal, to your pre-run breakfast as well. After this week there are only 6 weeks to go, which means only a handful of opportunities to get these important aspects of your race nailed down.

Be prepared to be challenged mentally as well as physically on Sunday. This is a very long way to run. Find your own mantra to help keep you going when you just don't feel like keeping on going. Remember why you are doing this. This is a very good session to do with a group of similar paced runners. Treat yourself after this one. Plan something nice for when it is done and it will give you something to look forward to while out running. Maybe it will be a long hot bath, going out for dinner, or even just relaxing the rest of the day. Plan ahead and look after yourself.

Weekly Volume: 36 miles (58k)

LSDR Distance: 20 miles (32k)

Week 14 Training Sessions - Total Volume: 36 miles (58k)

Day | Distance | Type of Run

Monday - 3 miles (5k) - Easy Run

Easy on the heart rate table so 60%-70% of max HR. This is a conversational pace and breathing should not be labored.

Tuesday - 6 miles (10k) - Easy Run

Easy on the heart rate table so 60%-70% of max HR. This is a conversational pace and breathing should not be labored.

Wednesday - No Running - N/A

No running days are perfect cross training days. Keep cross training relatively easy at this point in the training plan. If strength training, keep it at a level that won't impede your running ability in the days ahead.

Thursday - 4 miles (6k) - CoP Run

- 1 mile Easy (1.5k) +
- 2 miles Steady (3k) +
- 1 mile Easy (1.5k)

A Change of Pace run consists of an easy mile to start, followed by a mile at a slight change of pace faster and lastly 1 mile easy to finish it. The middle mile should be at a steady pace, a moderate heart rate, 70%-80% of max HR. This should feel comfortably hard, but still able to speak a few words at a time.

Friday - Rest Day - N/A

A rest day means no running or cross training. These are perfect days for extra stretching, yoga, or foam rolling.

Saturday - 3 miles (5k) - Easy Run

Easy on the heart rate table so 60%-70% of max HR. This is a conversational pace and breathing should not be labored.

Sunday - 20 miles (32k) - LSDR

The Long Slow Distance Run can be a zone 1 - zone 2 run, between 50%-70% max HR. This is the key run of the week and should be comfortable throughout. A great run to do alongside runners of similar ability.

WEEK 15

Focus: You are moving through this plan really well, keep up the impressive work. In week 15 there won't be anything new thrown your way. You have one CoP run and a slightly shorter LSDR. Your weekly running schedule is by now a habit and you should be well into your routine. Many of the non-running variables should be worked out, or close to being worked out, by now.

Weekly Volume: 37 miles (59k)

LSDR Distance: 17 miles (27k)

WEEK 15 TRAINING SESSIONS - TOTAL VOLUME: 37 miles (59k)

Day | Distance | Type of Run
Monday - 3 miles (5k) - Easy Run

Easy on the heart rate table so 60%-70% of max HR. This is a conversational pace and breathing should not be labored.

Tuesday - 5 miles (8k) - CoP Run

- 1 mile Easy (1.5k) +
- 3 miles Steady (5k) +
- 1 mile Easy (1.5k)

A Change of Pace run consists of an easy mile to start, followed by a mile at a slight change of pace faster and lastly 1 mile easy to finish it. The middle mile should be at a steady pace, a moderate heart rate, 70%-80% of max HR. This should feel comfortably hard, but still able to speak a few words at a time.

Wednesday - No Running - N/A

No running days are perfect cross training days. Keep cross training relatively easy at this point in the training plan. If strength training, keep it at a level that won't impede your running ability in the days ahead.

Thursday - 8 miles (13k) - Easy Run

Easy on the heart rate table so 60%-70% of max HR. This is a conversational pace and breathing should not be labored.

Friday - Rest Day - N/A

A rest day means no running or cross training. These are perfect days for extra stretching, yoga, or foam rolling.

Saturday - 4 miles (6k) - Easy Run

Easy on the heart rate table so 60%-70% of max HR. This is a conversational pace and breathing should not be labored.

Sunday - 17 miles (27k) - LSDR

The Long Slow Distance Run can be a zone 1 - zone 2 run, between 50%-70% max HR. This is the key run of the week and should be comfortable throughout. A great run to do alongside runners of similar ability.

WEEK 16

Focus: Week 16 is the last week of training in the Pace phase. This is where you can see where you are at with your training by doing another Yasso 800 session. It is a chance to check in and compare your results from this Yasso to the last time you did them in week 9. Are you completing them in the time you hoped to? If they are close, but not quite there, don't panic. Keep in mind that your body has been working very hard over the last four months. If you are close, then with a good Race phase of your training you should be on target. The key is to not try to work even harder now, just stick to the plan as it is. Extra work and fatigue on your muscles won't make you faster now. We will work on rebuilding during the next phase.

Weekly Volume: 37 miles (60k)
LSDR Distance: 18 miles (29k)

Week 16 Training Sessions - Total Volume: 37 miles (60k)

Day Distance Type of Run
Monday - 3 miles (5k) - Easy Run

Easy on the heart rate table so 60%-70% of max HR. This is a conversational pace and breathing should not be labored.

Tuesday - 5 miles (8k) - Yasso 800's

- 1 mile (1600m) easy +
- 6 reps x 800m with 400m walk/ slow jog recovery between reps +
- 1 mile (1600m) easy

This modified Yasso 800's session is an effective marathon-based interval session. The session consists of running 800m intervals. The pace to run these is calculated by taking the Goal Marathon Finish Time and converting it from hours and minutes to minutes and seconds. An example would be if the goal is to complete the marathon in 4 hours 30 minutes, then each 800m rep should be completed in 4 minutes and 30 seconds. Start the session with a 1-mile easy run warmup and finish it with a 1-mile easy cooldown

Wednesday - No Running - N/A

No running days are perfect cross training days. Keep cross training relatively easy at this point in the training plan. If strength training, keep it at a level that won't impede your running ability in the days ahead.

Thursday - 8 miles (13k) - Easy Run

Easy on the heart rate table so 60%-70% of max HR. This is a conversational pace and breathing should not be labored.

Friday - Rest Day - N/A

A rest day means no running or cross training. These are perfect days for extra stretching, yoga, or foam rolling.

Saturday - 3 miles (5k) - Easy Run

Easy on the heart rate table so 60%-70% of max HR. This is a conversational pace and breathing should not be labored.

Sunday - 18 miles (29k) - LSDR

The Long Slow Distance Run can be a zone 1 - zone 2 run, between 50%-70% max HR. This is the key run of the week and should be comfortable throughout. A great run to do alongside runners of similar ability.

THE RACE PHASE

Welcome to the first week of the Race phase of your first marathon program. In these next four weeks we will transition from building endurance and speed endurance to where we get you into a race-ready state. We will do more work for your mental fitness and preparedness in addition to running.

This does not mean the hard work is over. There is still your longest run in the program and still some challenging workouts. However, the closer to the event you get, the lighter the workload will be.

It is normal to feel tired and drained by this point. You have covered a lot of ground and traveled many miles over the past 16 weeks. You will be getting your body and mind in peak condition over these next four weeks. You are probably wishing this was the final week. Keep in mind that you are almost there. You may not feel it, but you will start to feel amazing in the upcoming weeks. Trust yourself and your training and know you will be race-fit and race-ready. You got this.

WEEK 17

Focus: This week you have your biggest run on your plan. You are going to get a 22 mile (35k) run as part of your race preparation. Everything should be worked out and this is the run to ensure all the little things are in place. Nutrition, hydration, and your sleep routine should be carried out as if this is race-day morning.

Starting this week, we are going to start working on our mental fitness. On Monday morning, when you wake up, but before your feet hit the ground, say either out loud or to yourself, "I am a marathoner. I am a strong marathon runner. My training has gone well. I am ready for this race." Say these, or similar words every single morning before you get out of bed. It may sound a bit woo-woo, but building a positive mindset is an extremely effective way to ensure a positive result in your event.

On your Sunday LSDR it is a great practice to use these same positive mantras to help you get through your run. When you feel tired and like you want to stop, use these statements to get you through that next stride, that next mile (km), that next 5k. Remind yourself why you are doing this and remember how much work you have put in. You are amazing to reach this point and know that at the end of this week there is only 3 weeks left before you reach the glory of doing something you may have thought you would never be able to do.

    Weekly Volume: 39 miles (62k)
    LSDR Distance: 22 miles (35k)

Week 17 Training Sessions - Total Volume: 39 miles (62k)

Day | Distance | Type of Run
Monday - 3 miles (5k) - Easy Run

Easy on the heart rate table so 60%-70% of max HR. This is a conversational pace and breathing should not be labored.

Tuesday - 4 miles (6k) - Easy Run

Easy on the heart rate table so 60%-70% of max HR. This is a conversational pace and breathing should not be labored.

Wednesday - No Running - N/A

No running days are perfect cross training days. Keep cross training relatively easy at this point in the training plan. If strength training, keep it at a level that won't impede your running ability in the days ahead.

Thursday - 5 miles (8k) - CoP Run

- 1 mile Easy (1.5k) +
- 3 miles Steady (5k) +
- 1 mile Easy (1.5k)

A Change of Pace run consists of an easy mile to start, followed by a mile at a slight change of pace faster and lastly 1 mile easy to finish it. The middle mile should be at a steady pace, a moderate heart rate, 70%-80% of max HR. This should feel comfortably hard, but still able to speak a few words at a time.

Friday - Rest Day - N/A

A rest day means no running or cross training. These are perfect days for extra stretching, yoga, or foam rolling.

Saturday - 5 miles (8k) - Easy Run

Easy on the heart rate table so 60%-70% of max HR. This is a conversational pace and breathing should not be labored.

Sunday - 22 miles (35k) - LSDR

The Long Slow Distance Run can be a zone 1 - zone 2 run, between 50%-70% max HR. This is the key run of the week and should be comfortable throughout. A great run to do alongside runners of similar ability.

Work on your mental fitness during this run. It is the

longest run in your program so remind yourself that you are a strong, fit and capable marathon runner. Use your mantras.

WEEK 18

Focus: We continue this week with the mental exercises you began last week. Make the positive self-talk part of your morning routine and throughout your entire day. There are some other positive things about this week. This is week one of your taper. The taper is where the weekly volume starts to come down, like a 3-week cut back before race day.

If you are traveling for your race, this is a good week to ensure your accommodation plans are set in stone and it is advisable to make pre-race dinner reservations. If your race is of any significant size, then Italian restaurants in the area will likely fill up fast and it may be difficult to get a dinner reservation at your preferred time. I always plan my dinner reservations to be a half-hour before the time I like to eat. That gives time to order and have the meal prepared.

You should have breakfast plans in place as well, but this will be far better if you handle it in your room, or accommodation, yourself so as to not leave anything up to chance. This is especially true if you have any special dietary requirements or if you have an early start and like to eat a couple of hours before you run. Just think ahead and be prepared.

Weekly Volume: 31 miles (50k)

LSDR Distance: 16 miles (26k)

Week 18 Training Sessions - Total Volume: 31 miles (50k)

Day | Distance | Type of Run
Monday - 3 miles (5k) - Easy Run

Easy on the heart rate table so 60%-70% of max HR. This is a conversational pace and breathing should not be labored.

Tuesday - 5 miles (8k) - CoP Run

- 1 mile Easy (1.5k) +
- 3 miles Steady (5k) +
- 1 mile Easy (1.5k)

A Change of Pace run consists of an easy mile to start, followed by a mile at a slight change of pace faster and lastly 1 mile easy to finish it. The middle mile should be at a steady pace, a moderate heart rate, 70%-80% of max HR. This should feel comfortably hard, but still able to speak a few words at a time.

Wednesday - No Running - N/A

No running days are perfect cross training days. Keep cross training relatively easy at this point in the training plan. If strength training, keep it at a level that won't impede your running ability in the days ahead.

Thursday - 4 miles (6k) - Hilly Run

Choose an undulating route that includes at least one tough hill in it. Hill training is a great all-around workout that trains strength, aerobic capacity, and endurance.

Friday - Rest Day - N/A

A rest day means no running or cross training. These are perfect days for extra stretching, yoga, or foam rolling.

Saturday - 3 miles (5k) - Easy Run

Easy on the heart rate table so 60%-70% of max HR. This is a conversational pace and breathing should not be labored.

Sunday - 16 miles (26k) - LSDR

The Long Slow Distance Run can be a zone 1 - zone 2 run, between 50%-70% max HR. This is the key run of the week and should be comfortable throughout. A great run to do alongside runners of similar ability.

WEEK 19

Focus: Only 2-weeks left. You are most likely just waiting for this whole process to be over and done with. But it is important that you give yourself all the credit you deserve for sticking with this plan and getting this far. It is hard, which is why not everybody does it. But you have nearly completed all of the necessary training and you *will* complete your first marathon. It is no longer a question of *can I do it*, it is now a statement of *I will do it*!

In addition to your positive self-talk, which you should continue to do every day, you will be adding another mental exercise. From here on out, take 2-3 minutes, every day, and sit somewhere quiet, close your eyes and see yourself crossing the finish line with your desired time on the clock. Hear the crowd along the course as you run past them. Feel the volunteer putting the hard-earned medal around your neck. Visualize yourself celebrating with your family and friends when it is all done. Once again, much like positive self-talk, visualization is a highly effective mental tool that can be used to your advantage as you prepare for your first marathon. I like to compare it to a golfer or a football player. These professional athletes stand over their shots, or kicks, and visualize the ball going exactly where they want it to go. See it and make it happen. You will be doing the same thing, only in your chosen sport.

It is important to also prepare for the difficult moments in your race. Being mentally prepared for how you will push through when the going gets hard. Miles 20 onward may very well feel tough. Visualize yourself persevering and powering on. See the mile markers going by and know that every step is another step closer to the finish line. When you face these moments on the course, you are far more likely to get through them with resilience and brute force.

One more thing to think about is this is the week to check in on your feet. Do you need to cut your toenails, or if you'd prefer, get a pedicure. Do you have corns or calluses that need to be addressed? Don't wait until next week to handle these tasks.

It is normal to start feeling phantom pains or to be overly anxious about getting sick. Do your best to put these things out of your mind. Getting sick or picking up an injury can happen, but it is unlikely, and worrying will only give you unnecessary anxiety. Just live as you did the previous 18 weeks. Make good decisions, keeping your race in mind. The unusual or new pains you are feeling are probably because your workload is decreasing and your body feels "different" than it did. Stay relaxed and keep yourself busy during the times you aren't running. You will be grateful for having something to occupy your mind. I like to do some gentle walking to help me keep focussed. During these walks there is time to work on the mental exercises we've been doing.

Weekly Volume: 26 miles (42k)

LSDR Distance: 13 miles (21k)

WEEK 19 TRAINING SESSIONS - TOTAL VOLUME: 26 MILES (42K)

Day | Distance | Type of Run
Monday - 3 miles (5k) - Easy Run

Easy on the heart rate table so 60%-70% of max HR. This is a conversational pace and breathing should not be labored.

Tuesday - 3 miles (5k) - CoP Run

- 1 mile Easy (1.5k) +
- 1 mile Steady (2k) +
- 1 mile Easy (1.5k)

A Change of Pace run consists of an easy mile to start, followed by a mile at a slight change of pace faster and lastly 1 mile easy to finish it. The middle mile should be at a steady pace, a moderate heart rate, 70%-80% of max HR. This should feel comfortably hard, but still able to speak a few words at a time.

Wednesday - No Running - N/A

No running days are perfect cross training days. Keep cross training relatively easy at this point in the training plan. If strength training, keep it at a level that won't impede your running ability in the days ahead.

Thursday - 3 miles (5k) - CoP Run

- 1 mile Easy (1.5k) +

- 1 mile Steady (2k) +
- 1 mile Easy (1.5k)

A Change of Pace run consists of an easy mile to start, followed by a mile at a slight change of pace faster and lastly 1 mile easy to finish it. The middle mile should be at a steady pace, a moderate heart rate, 70%-80% of max HR. This should feel comfortably hard, but still able to speak a few words at a time.

Friday - Rest Day - N/A

A rest day means no running or cross training. These are perfect days for extra stretching, yoga, or foam rolling.

Saturday - 4 miles (6k) - Easy Run

Easy on the heart rate table so 60%-70% of max HR. This is a conversational pace and breathing should not be labored.

Sunday - 13 miles (21k) - LSDR

The Long Slow Distance Run can be a zone 1 - zone 2 run, between 50%-70% max HR. This is the key run of the week and should be comfortable throughout. A great run to do alongside runners of similar ability.

WEEK 20

Focus: Finally, you have arrived at race week. Keep working on positive self-talk and visualization. In addition, think about getting your haircut, buy some new clothes for going out after the race, get a spray tan, a spa session, or some other reward for putting in all the work. Much like going to a job interview, if you feel good about how you look, you will have more confidence in how you perform. Look good, feel good, perform good.

You only have 8 miles prior to race day. Run them relaxed, knowing that these are just to keep your legs turning over. You are prepared and now you just want your body to be fully recovered from all the work you put in. You will get no benefit from any hard training now, so smile and be extremely proud of yourself.

Weekly Volume: 34.2 miles (55.2k) – Includes the Marathon Event

LSDR Distance: 26.2 miles (42.2k) – The Marathon Event

Week 20 Training Sessions - Total Volume: 34.2 miles (55.2k)

Day | Distance | Type of Run
Monday - 3 miles (5k) - Easy Run

Easy on the heart rate table so 60%-70% of max HR. This is a conversational pace and breathing should not be labored.

Tuesday - Rest Day - N/A

A rest day means no running or cross training. These are perfect days for extra stretching, yoga, or foam rolling.

Wednesday - 3 miles (5k) - Easy Run

Easy on the heart rate table so 60%-70% of max HR. This is a conversational pace and breathing should not be labored.

Thursday - Rest Day - N/A

A rest day means no running or cross training. These are perfect days for extra stretching, yoga, or foam rolling.

Friday - Rest Day - N/A

A rest day means no running or cross training. These are perfect days for extra stretching, yoga, or foam rolling.

Saturday - 2 miles (3k) - Easy Run

This is just an easy run to remind you that you are a runner and tomorrow you transition into a marathoner.

Sunday - 26.2 (42.2k) - **Race Day**

Enjoy everything about your race. You have done everything possible to prepare and it will show. Soak in the crowds, the noise, the excitement. Read the funny posters and high-five all the kids holding out their hands. Have fun! You deserve this and have earned this medal!

POST RACE CARE

You are a marathon runner now. How amazing is that? What comes next? Well, to be honest, you are not done yet. You've seen the comedy sketches showing runners hobbling around after running a marathon, taking ages to go up or down stairs, quite gingerly mind you. You can now sympathize with these people. From the moment you cross the line and receive your medal you are going to notice a significant change in your body's ability to move in a coherent fashion.

Don't worry, this is normal. The best thing you can do after the race is keep moving. Keep walking to the bag drop area and pick up your things. Put your warm clothes on, get something to drink and keep moving. If at all possible, do some stretching, even just a little bit, particularly the most sore and stiff areas of your body.

When you do find a place to sit, if your stomach can handle it, try to take onboard something to eat. Many races will have tents and volunteers giving out snacks. Oftentimes you will get bananas or other fruit. These are excellent sources of energy after your marathon. Some kind of protein source would be advisable as well. Remember, you just beat up your muscles for a very long time over a very long distance. Be kind to them.

Inevitably, many runners will want to celebrate with alcohol after the marathon. This is OK, but try to keep it in moderation. Alcohol is not the best recovery method and it will hit twice as hard as it normally would. You have just made plenty of sacrifices over the past 16 - 20 weeks, my advice is to hang in there for one more day. Celebrate for sure, but do so sensibly. Get a full day of recovery and then splurge on the food and drinks you missed out on during the training cycle. You will not regret this decision.

After a good night's sleep, the DOMS will certainly start to kick in. There is a massive benefit to going for a short, very slow jog the day after the marathon. By doing this, you are increasing the blood flow to your sore leg muscles and loosening them up. Even two miles will be helpful. By the time you get two miles done, you will most likely find that everything feels a little better.

Definitely take a few days off after this and avoid any kind of speedy run for at least a week. The best is yet to come. After at least two weeks and ideally in the third week after the marathon, you will find yourself in extremely good condition to take on a 5k or 10k race and absolutely smash it. All the miles and hard work is still there and the best thing is that the shorter distance will *feel* easy to you.

Bask in the glory of being a marathoner for the rest of your life and go crush some personal records in the shorter distances over the next few months. Also, it is important to just run for the joy of running. It's not all about chasing times and achievements. Sometimes running is just what our mind and body needs to just get through another day and another week.

So from here, I'd like to say, it has been an amazing adventure to take you through your first marathon. I've enjoyed sharing my experience and expertise in marathon running with you. I hope you enjoyed the experience and the accomplishment. If you did, I would very much appreciate it if you would spread the word about me and my books. Please do look me up on social media and reach out. I'd love to hear how you got on.

CONGRATULATIONS

You've done it!

If you enjoyed *Running Your First Marathon Made EASY, All the Secrets You Need to Know for First Marathon SUCCESS,* **please leave a positive review of this book on Amazon or wherever you purchased it**. It is so important to coaches and authors who are producing quality work for distribution. It is a great way for this book to be put in front of more people.

I've enjoyed working with you and please look for more of my books and training programs by browsing Amazon. You will find more books for the beginners and intermediate runners in your life. These offer easy to follow programs for hitting distance and speed goals. For now, bask in the greatness of what you just achieved. I am proud of you and you should be proud of yourself!

CONGRATULATIONS

ADDITIONAL RESOURCES

Browse all my books on the following pages or on my Amazon author page.

If you are interested in learning more about the author or need some additional inspiration, my memoir A Heart for Running: How Running Saved My Life is available on Amazon.

Other Books & Social Media

Browse all on my books Amazon author page.

If you are interested in learning more about the my life experience or need some additional inspiration, my memoir A Heart for Running: How Running Saved My Life is available on Amazon.

There are also all of the usual social media suspects, each of which is listed below.

I would very much like to hear from you with feedback. I am extremely interested in your results from your target marathon. Please provide some feedback on one of the following links:

Facebook - https://facebook.com/johnmcdonnell.runningcoach
Instagram - https://instagram.com/jmruncoach
YouTube - https://youtube.com/@jmruncoach

I also have a blog dedicated to my personal running and life experiences at A Heart for Running. I take great interest in all runners and would love to hear from you, so please do reach out in one form or another.

PERSONAL COACHING

Putting together a training program that will suit every first time marathoner is a tall order. Not everyone has the same work schedule, family commitments, running experience, etc. If at any point you find this whole experience of getting prepared to run your first marathon a little overwhelming, and it often is, you are not alone, and I am able to help.

I have coached hundreds of marathoners, including so many tackling their first marathon that I've lost count. It is an especially rewarding experience for me when a runner accomplishes something that once seemed impossible. For many people, that is precisely what a marathon is, a bucket list aspiration. Spreading my passion for marathoning is something I pride myself in.

Some runners need an extra little push in order to stay true to their goals. Someone to hold them accountable. Someone to adjust their plans when injuries and niggles start creeping in. Someone to answer questions on a daily or

PERSONAL COACHING

weekly basis and explain the ins-and-outs of the training. I work with runners of every ability from the complete beginner to the advanced runner, all at less than the price of your daily coffee.

Discover a personalized approach to elevate your running journey with my coaching services. Embrace a monthly coaching package featuring comprehensive support: receive weekly training updates, engage in regular video call check-ins, and access unlimited guidance to address all your inquiries and worries. While books and guides provide valuable insights, nothing parallels the impact of individualized coaching. Benefit from tailored training plans geared towards specific races or maintaining peak performance between events.

Moreover, within these coaching packages, you'll discover choices for strength training regimens and personalized meal plans. Running holds transformative power, and these all-encompassing coaching packages aim to sculpt you into the well-rounded athlete you aspire to be. Explore your diverse coaching options today at https://jmruncoach.com/.

If you are ready to elevate your running and crush new personal records then sign up today. Or you can also reach out to me at John McDonnell Running Coach on Facebook and we can discuss your goals and how I can help you reach them. I am also contactable by email at john@jmruncoach.com. One way or the other, I'd love to hear from you. Feedback on my books is always appreciated.

ACKNOWLEDGMENTS

No book is ever written in isolation, especially a coaching book. It takes input and experience from a variety of sources. It also takes a commitment from friends and family alike. I'd like to take this opportunity to thank every member of my family. You all contribute to my success as a coach and as a runner in your own way. I wouldn't be the person I am today without each of you.

I'd also like to thank all of the athletes who put their trust in me to help them reach their goals. I have learned so much from each coaching opportunity and experience. I have had the great pleasure of working with some of the strongest and mentally tough athlete's I've ever met. You inspire me to continue to learn and also to push myself.

In particular, a big thank you to Glenda and Pauline who gave me permission to use their first marathon experiences as case studies in this book. I had the honor of coaching them through their first marathons and they both came through the program with flying colors. I am so proud of both of you and grateful for your commitment and perseverance.

I'd like to thank Carleth Keys who has become a running friend in Spain. Although we live on opposite sides of this large country, we stay in touch and make the effort to run together.

Lastly, to all my running friends, new and old. We share the ability to do hard things and I am grateful every day to share this wonderful sport with you.

Best of luck to everyone in your running adventures. If our paths happen to cross, please reach out and make yourself known. I'd love to meet you in person.

ALSO BY JOHN MCDONNELL

Marathon Training Strategies: A Comprehensive Guide to Running Your Best Marathon - Including Plans, Advice, and Goal-Hitting Tips

Unlock the Secrets to Marathon Success

Every step you take in the world of marathon running is a journey toward the extraordinary. The marathon is more than a race; it's a test of your willpower, endurance, and determination. To conquer the marathon and achieve your personal best, you need more than just physical strength – you need a comprehensive strategy that encompasses both body and mind. In "Marathon Training Strategies," John delves into the art and science of marathon preparation, equipping you with the knowledge, motivation, and training plans to cross the finish line in your personal best time.

Your Roadmap to Marathon Mastery

This book is not just another training guide; it's your roadmap to marathon mastery. Drawing on years of experience and expertise, John has crafted six distinct training plans, each tailored to help you reach a specific goal:

Sub 2:45 Marathon: For the elite runners striving for greatness.

Sub 3-Hour Marathon: An ambitious goal for those seeking to join the ranks of the sub-3 club.

Sub 3:15 Marathon: A challenging yet achievable target for serious runners.

Sub 3:30 Marathon: A goal that pushes the boundaries of endurance.

Sub 3:45 Marathon: Perfect for runners who want to excel while balancing life's demands.

Sub 4-Hour Marathon: A realistic plan for dedicated runners who want to conquer the marathon.

But "Marathon Training Strategies" is more than just training plans; it's a holistic approach to marathon preparation. He understands running a marathon isn't just about physical fitness, it's also about mental fortitude.

Your Training Companion

Within these pages, you'll discover:

Proven Training Plans: John's meticulously designed training plans are backed by science and years of experience. John's plans cater to your needs, ensuring that you're well-prepared for race day.

Nutrition and Hydration: Fueling your body is essential for marathon success. Learn how to optimize your nutrition and hydration to keep your energy levels high and your body primed for peak performance.

Injury Prevention: Running long distances can take a toll on your body. Discover effective injury prevention techniques and recovery strategies to keep you in top form throughout your training.

Mental Toughness: The marathon is as much a mental challenge as a physical one. Gain insights into visualization techniques, goal-setting strategies, and mental toughness exercises to overcome those challenging moments.

Race Day Strategies: When it comes to race day, every detail matters. From pacing and fueling to dealing with the unexpected, John guides you through the intricacies of marathon racing.

The Journey Begins Here

Whether you're aiming for a sub-2:45 marathon or striving to break the 4-hour barrier, "Marathon Training Strategies" is your trusted companion on this epic quest. It won't be easy, but it will certainly be worth it. The marathon is a test of your limits, a quest for personal excellence, and an opportunity to prove to yourself that you can achieve greatness.

"Marathon Training Strategies" is your ticket to marathon success. It's time to lace up your running shoes, set your sights on the finish line, and let this comprehensive guide be your guiding light on the path to running your best marathon ever.

Your Marathon Journey Starts Now.

Order your copy of "Marathon Training Strategies: A Comprehensive Guide to Running Your Best Marathon - Including Plans, Advice, and Goal-Hitting Tips" and unlock the secrets to marathon success today.

A Heart for Running: How Running Saved My Life

In 2010, John McDonnell wasn't a runner; he was just an ordinary guy leading an ordinary life. Until one fateful day, when he stumbled upon vacation photos that revealed a stark truth – he had become overweight. Determined to reclaim his health and vitality, he embarked on a journey that would forever alter the course of his life: he started running.

What began as a quest to shed pounds quickly evolved into an unrelenting passion for running. John's transformation was nothing short of remarkable; he transitioned from 5K races to conquering 10K, half-marathons, and ultimately, the full marathon. Each step was fueled by an insatiable desire for self-improvement, and it became evident that running was his lifeline.

In 2017, adversity struck in the form of a devastating stroke, a dire consequence of an unsuspecting 11mm hole in his heart. For many, this setback might have marked the end of the road, but not for John. With unwavering determination and sheer grit, he embarked on a journey to reclaim his life once more.

"A Heart for Running" is more than just a running memoir; it's a testament to the incredible power of the human spirit. John's story is one of dedication, passion, and relentless perseverance. It's about defying the odds, refusing to succumb to setbacks, and emerging stronger on the other side.

Could John fulfill his dream of making a full comeback in the sport that had not only transformed his physique but also saved his life? Follow his emotional rollercoaster as he races against time and physical barriers, all in pursuit of the elusive 3-hour marathon barrier. His journey unfolds with raw honesty and humor, inviting you into his world of sweat, triumphs, and occasional misadventures.

Throughout "A Heart for Running," John invites you to share in his experiences, spanning over 30 marathons across Ireland, the UK, and beyond. From the exhilarating highs of crossing finish lines to the humbling lows of cramps and exhaustion, his storytelling paints a vivid picture of the runner's life.

Join John in this inspiring memoir, where the finish line is just the beginning of a new challenge, and where every step is a testament to the incredible potential within us all. "A Heart for Running" is not just a running book; it's a reminder that no obstacle is insurmountable, and that the journey is as extraordinary as the destination.

Experience the highs, lows, and the indomitable spirit of a man who refused to be defined by his setbacks. Discover the power of running to heal, transform, and ultimately transcend the limits of what's possible. John's journey is an inspiration to us all, proving that no matter your age, circumstances, or previous experience, the road ahead is yours to conquer.

What People Are Saying:

"**Plot/Idea:** McDonnell's perseverance is contagious. His honest approach to his process will inspire others to get off the couch and hit the pavement. While we often think of those that are ranked athletes as people who are physically gifted in some way, McDonnell proves that this is not the case with his compelling story and approach to his hard work.

Prose: McDonnell's compelling story is easy to read and highly inspirational. His encouraging personality shines through his writing.

Character/Execution: The level of detail McDonnell offers, notably, about his training schedule and techniques, proves to be a benefit for readers aspiring to challenge themselves physically." - The BookLife Prize

"An amazing read, relatable, thought provoking and lessons for us all to remember what is truly important!" - **Teresa McDaid - Athletics Ireland**

"A Heart for Running is an emotional rollercoaster, and you feel every single moment with John. Running quite literally saved his life and his story is an inspiration and a beacon of hope for us all." - **Irish Runner Magazine**

Running for Beginners: The Easiest Guide to Running Your First 5K In Only 6 Weeks

Unlock Your Inner Runner and Achieve the Impossible

Have you ever watched a marathon or a local 5k race and felt that deep-seated desire to join the ranks of those fleet-footed runners, to feel the exhilaration of crossing the finish line? You're not alone. Running has a unique allure, a primal call to push your limits, and discover what your body and mind are truly capable of. But where do you start? How do you go from being a non-runner to someone who can confidently run a 5k race without stopping? The answer lies within the pages of "Running for Beginners."

In this comprehensive and easy-to-follow guide, John, a seasoned runner and experienced coach, takes you on a transformative journey from complete novice to a confident 5k finisher in just 6 weeks. Whether you're an absolute beginner or someone who hasn't laced up running shoes in years, this book is your roadmap to success.

A Guided Journey to 5k Success

John understands the challenges that beginners face because he's been there himself. He knows the doubts, the fears, and the questions that can hold you back. That's why he's crafted this book to be your ultimate companion, offering guidance, motivation, and a step-by-step plan to turn your running aspirations into reality.

Inside "Running for Beginners," you'll discover:

Week-by-Week Training Plans: John has designed a 6-week training program that gradually builds your endurance and stamina. Each week, you'll receive clear instructions on when, where, and how far to run. The plan is tailored for beginners, ensuring that you progress at a pace that's comfortable for you.

Coaching Tips from an Expert: John's coaching expertise shines through in his advice on form, technique, and injury prevention. You'll learn how to run efficiently and avoid common mistakes that new runners often make.

The Basics You Need to Know: From choosing the right running shoes to understanding proper nutrition and hydration, "Running for Beginners" covers all the essential elements of becoming a successful runner.

Mental Toughness: Running is not just a physical endeavor; it's a mental one too. John shares strategies to help you stay motivated, overcome mental barriers, and develop the mental fortitude needed to complete your first 5k.

A Community of Runners: Join a community of like-minded individuals who are on their own running journeys. Connect with others, share your progress, and find the support you need to stay motivated and accountable.

Your Journey Starts Today

Imagine the feeling of accomplishment as you cross the finish line of your first 5k race. Picture the smiles, cheers, and sense of pride that await you. With "Running for Beginners" as your guide, that dream can become your reality. This book is not just about running; it's about discovering your true potential and proving to yourself that you can achieve anything you set your mind to.

Are you ready to take that first step, to put on your running shoes and embark on a journey that will change your life? The road to becoming a runner starts right here, right now. Join John and countless others who have transformed themselves through the power of running. It's time to lace up, hit the pavement, and make your first 5k race a reality.

Your First 5k Awaits.

Order your copy of "Running for Beginners: The Easiest Guide to Running Your First 5k in Only 6 Weeks" and begin your journey to becoming a confident and accomplished runner today.

Step Up to 10k: Improve Your 5k Time and Train for a 10k

Elevate Your Running Journey from 5K to 10K

Ready to transform your running prowess after conquering the 5K? "Step Up to 10K" is your comprehensive guide to becoming a 10K champion. Crafted by a seasoned running coach, this book unveils advanced training techniques and expert insights to help you reach new heights in your running endeavors.

As you embark on this exhilarating journey, you'll discover the keys to mastering both uphill and downhill terrains, thanks to our comprehensive coaching tips. Dive deep into the world of interval training, learn to harness the power of tempo runs, and embark on progressions that will propel your running prowess to new horizons.

Whether you're in your first or second year of training, this book is meticulously designed to ensure a seamless transition from 5K to 10K. But it doesn't stop there. Our specially designed training plan isn't just about conquering the 10K; it's about turbocharging your 5K performance as well, making this the year of personal records.

Your Guide to Running Excellence

"Step Up to 10K" is more than just a book; it's your portal to cutting-edge running expertise. Throughout these pages, you'll find access to exclusive video guides on essential topics like breathing techniques, dynamic drills, and post-run stretching – all aimed at optimizing your performance and preventing injuries.

Your running journey is about more than just races; it's about personal growth, resilience, and achieving feats you once thought impossible. This book is your trusted companion on this journey, offering guidance and motivation every step of the way.

Transform Your Running Experience

Transform your 10K journey into an immensely rewarding experience. With "Step Up to 10K" as your trusted companion, your running goals are well within reach. Whether you're conquering new distances or chasing personal bests, this guide has got you covered.

It's time to lace up your running shoes, set your sights on new horizons, and make this year one filled with remarkable achievements. Whether you're a novice or an experienced runner, "Step Up to 10K" will take your running to the next level.

Don't wait any longer. Elevate your running journey to new heights, and unlock your full running potential. Make this year the year you become a 10K champion.

"Step Up to 10K: Improve Your 5k Time and Train for a 10k" – your ultimate key to running greatness.

The Achieve More Running Journal

The **"Achieve More" Running Journal: A Comprehensive Statistics Diary and Race Planner to Inspire and Help Achieve All Your Running Goals** is the perfect gift for any runner. It is used to track all the statistics to help inspire progress in running and fitness.

"If you can't measure it, you can't improve it." - Peter Drucker

By measuring all the vital statistics a runner needs like daily and weekly sleep, daily and weekly calorie intake, water intake, heart rate, etc., every runner will find the missing links in their running. Improvements are made easier when we see what needs to be improved. This journal tracks annual target races, running gear purchases, race entries, personal bests in every race distance.

There are templates to fill in training plans of up to 16 weeks at a time, track injuries and recoveries, and so much more:

- Sleep
- Heart Rate
- Calorie Consumption
- Water Consumption
- Trainers & Gear Purchased
- How Each Run Felt
- Weekly Summaries & Averages
- So Much More...

Make this the best running year for yourself or someone you love with this unique running journal.